light
your home

elizabeth wilhide

COLLINS|DESIGN
An Imprint of HarperCollinsPublishers

First Edition

First published in 2005 by:
Collins Design,
An Imprint of HarperCollins*Publishers*
10 East 53rd Street
New York, NY 10022

Tel.: (212) 207-7000
Fax: (212) 207-7654
collinsdesign@harpercollins.com
www.harpercollins.com

Distributed throughout the world by:
HarperCollins *Publishers*
10 East 53rd Street
New York, NY 10022
Fax: (212) 207-7654

Director: Lorraine Dickey
Art Director: Jonathan Christie
Executive Editor: Zia Mattocks
Designer: Lucy Gowans
Editor: Sian Parkhouse
Picture Research Manager: Liz Boyd
Production Manager: Angela Couchman

Library of Congress Control Number: 2005927189
ISBN 0-06-083307-6

Printed in China
First printing, 2005

To Jenny

Contents

contents

Light describes the world to us. We see things because light reveals them and we move through spaces shaped by light and shade. At the same time, light taps deeply into our subconscious, summoning up powerful feelings of celebration, wellbeing and even spirituality – it is no accident that religious festivals from many different cultures, such as Christmas, Hanukkah and Divali, are all celebrated with light. Magical, mysterious, life-enhancing, light is one of the most evocative elements in interior design.

When it comes to designing a lighting scheme for the home environment, the minimum requirement is that it must work – that is the bottom line. That is to say, lighting should adequately fulfil its practical role and support everyday activities and routines after dark or whenever natural light levels are too low. It should be bright enough to allow us to perform the task at hand safely and comfortably, it should be flexible enough to allow for repositioning or dimming where necessary, and it should meet these basic requirements without causing glare while doing so.

Practicality, however, is only part of the picture. It is the emotive and associative aspects of lighting that are every bit as important as the functional role it must play. While it is always tempting to hold up natural light as the ultimate point of comparison for artificial lighting, the ideal to strive toward, in this context such a comparison can be misleading. Ever since early humans lit fires in the mouths of their caves, we have effectively spent at least part of our lives in conditions of 'artificial' light. First came firelight and candlelight; then came other sources of illumination such as oil and gas lamps. Eventually, at the end of the nineteenth century, Edison brought us the incandescent bulb and rapidly ushered in a new electric age.

As biological creatures, we need natural light and plenty of it – more, perhaps, than we experience today in a modern society where much of life and work happens indoors. On the other hand, as social creatures, we have an emotional need for the softer, dimmer light that artificial sources offer. Lower indoor light levels provide a sense of security and help to foster the

Above: *An electric field celebrates the mystery and potency of light. Richard Box, artist in residence at Bristol University, created this installation in 2004. In a field east of Bristol, 1,300 fluorescent tubes were stuck in the ground, their light powered solely by the electromagnetic field around overhead power cables.*

troduction

sense of community that supports relationships and family life. In fact, the notion of the home as a shelter and refuge is at least partially defined in our minds by artificial sources of light, however outmoded – the flickering flames in the hearth, the shaded reading lamp, the bedside light, the candles on the dining table – as points of intimacy and focus.

If artificial light should not be seen as a direct supplement to natural light, neither should it be assumed that the role of one is simply to take over from the other once darkness has fallen. In practice, natural and artificial light are forced to work together for long periods of the day. It is the mediation between the light that shines in through windows and other openings and the artificial lighting that we rely upon to perform everyday activities indoors, which forms the basis of every lighting scheme.

That our contemporary taste tends towards interiors as light-filled as possible might be considered a direct result of advances in technology which have increasingly made this possible, both in terms of improvements to light sources and in terms of the new structural possibilities of glass. Yet attitudes to light in the interior, both natural and artificial, have always shifted, and often for reasons that have had little to do with technical progress.

For many centuries, people had very little choice but to put up with relatively dim conditions indoors. Candles were an expensive item for most households. Early glass was cloudy and rippled and could be made only in small sizes; hence the typical northern European form of the casement window, leaded with many small lights. It has been suggested that one of the reasons why glass- and mirror-making reached such a height of sophistication in Venice was the need to transmit, reflect and refract as much light as possible in a city where narrow houses are densely crowded together. The same expertise was also to play a role in scientific enquiry. The invention of 'crystallo', a very beautiful and transparent glass, in sixteenth-century Venice, was a critical step in the development of the first spy glasses, early forms of telescopes where light was the vehicle for delivering valuable and hitherto inaccessible information about the heavens.

By the seventeenth and eighteenth centuries, when glass had dramatically improved in transparency and larger-sized panes could be produced, it was fashionable for interiors to be as light and bright as possible – fashionable

Opposite: *'The Weather Project' by Danish-Icelandic artist Olafur Eliasson transfixed some 2.3 million visitors to the Tate Modern gallery, London, in 2003–4. The centrepiece of the five-month exhibition was the installation of a hypnotic 'sun' in the vast Turbine Hall entranceway. The ceiling was covered with reflective foil and the 'sun' itself was made of glass and 144 low-sodium lights. The effect was to generate a remarkable sense of wellbeing in spectators who lounged and relaxed on the floor as if they were sunbathing in the open.*

because large windows were expensive (and taxable at certain points during this period) and because light was an obvious metaphor for an age devoted to reason and enquiry. After dark, chandeliers, candelabra and mirrors created sparkling theatrical displays where the wealthy could show off their riches and status. A hundred years later, with the Victorian preference for sombre, light-excluding decoration and furnishings, the reverse was the case. Darkened rooms, shrouded against the penetration of natural light, were evidence of refinement and soulful sensibility. With productive work increasingly taking place outside the home, the moody interior proclaimed its occupant as one of the leisured, cultured classes.

In the early twentieth century, when electric light first became widely available, it was immediately perceived to be dazzling and glaring in contrast to candlelight or gaslight, much dimmer and gentler sources of illumination.

As a result, it was not long before a lighting industry sprang up, creating fittings that not only supported or housed the bulb but also shaded it.

Today, our greatest luxury is space. Lighting is naturally space-enhancing and can make even restricted surroundings seem more expansive (and expensive) than they really are. Natural light, with its associations with health and holiday periods spent outdoors, also carries with it an undertone of privilege. However, in the pursuit of lightness and brightness, it can be possible to go too far. While we may no longer welcome Stygian Victorian gloom, when homes are overlit we run the risk of robbing interiors of all mystery and atmosphere. Even, diffused illumination may be effective in terms of function, but a vital dimension is missing, which is the animating quality of contrast and modelling that comes with shadow.

If light effects are subject to taste, the same is true of fittings. During the twentieth century, the design of light fittings has progressed from concealing the bulb to concealing the fitting itself. Early light fittings, which so often echoed candlesticks and gas lamps in form, remained decorative objects even when not switched on, which is perhaps why they were increasingly banished as homes became more clean-lined and minimal. Until recently, hidden or recessed lighting was the norm in contemporary interiors. Light was a visible presence glowing from the smooth planes of walls and ceilings; the fitting had been relegated to functional kit concealed from view. The proliferation of downlights, fittings originally used in the commercial and retail sector, has been a marked feature of this trend.

In the past few years, all this has changed and light fittings have become visible again. The recent resurgence of the chandelier is a case in

point. With sophisticated lighting systems, we have no need of the chandelier in a practical sense, but its ability to create a lighting spectacle has been sorely missed. Nowadays, sculptural lights, designs that blur the boundary between light and object, and light-emitting surfaces and finishes extend the notion of decorative lighting into an entirely new realm.

Today, we have an incredible breadth of choice when it comes to lighting the interior, not only of fixtures and fittings, but also of light sources themselves. Technologies such as fibre optics and LEDs (light-emitting diodes), which were marginal a decade ago, are on the cusp of becoming mainstream, while the future promises further advances with light-emitting materials and fabrics.

There has never been a more exciting time to Light Your Home.

Below: *The traditional Chinese Lantern Festival falls on the first full moon of the lunar new year. Here, Taiwanese people in Taipei release lanterns in the belief that they will bring good luck and blessings.*
Opposite: *'Cloud' pendant light by Jess Shaw, a billowing chandelier constructed from light strings and woven nylon tubing, was originally commissioned for the Frieze Art Fair by the British Council in Tokyo.*

practical

Lighting is supremely atmospheric, evocative and mood-enhancing. At the same time, it also has a crucial practical role to play, enabling us to work and function effectively when natural light levels are low or in hours of darkness. This section looks at the basics of practical lighting – how much is needed and where – so you can begin to devise a scheme that will suit your own home and individual requirements.

lighting

Assessing your needs

A good starting point when it comes to devising a lighting scheme is to consider exactly how much light you require. Technically speaking, light is measured in 'lux' levels (or 'footcandles' in the United States), which equate not to the amount of light emitted from a source but to the amount of light that arrives at a particular surface. Different lux levels are recommended for carrying out different types of activity. The following table provides a useful means of comparison.

Outdoor lux levels

Twilight	10 lux (1 ftcd)
Very dark day	107 lux (10 ftcd)
Overcast	1,075 lux (100 ftcd)
Daylight	10,750 lux (1,000 ftcd)
Bright sunlight	107,500 lux (10,000 ftcd)

Indoor lux levels

Minimum for safe movement	50 lux
Dimmed theatre	100 lux
Living area	200 lux
General work areas, eg kitchens	300–500 lux
Reading and desk work	500–750 lux
Drawing and detailed work	1,000–1,500 lux

On a clear sunny day an outdoor reading of 10,000 lux may be as much as ten times lower taken by a window indoors. Depending on the size of the space and how it is decorated and finished, that level might well decrease to 50 lux in dark corners or unlit parts of the room. The measurement of lux levels is essential for professional lighting designers who are charged with coming up with unique lighting schemes for shop interiors, auditoriums or workplaces. While the calculations are less critical when planning home lighting, you can always hire a lux meter for a reasonable cost if you would like to make more specific comparisons between different areas in your home. By and large, however, what is important to bear in mind is simply that the amount of light required will depend on the activity in question. A kitchen, for example, that was lit only to the same level as a living area would be a hazardous place in which to work.

Another important variable when it comes to lighting needs is age. The older we get, the more light we need to see comfortably by: at the age of 40, it is three times that of the average 10-year-old, and at 60, it's 15 times as much. If you wear glasses or have any sort of visual impairment, that requirement will also be increased.

SAD

Seasonal affective disorder is estimated to affect half a million people in Britain alone. Once dismissed as a fictional condition, recent empirical studies have suggested that it is a real problem for many people, occurring chiefly in northern latitudes and peaking between December and February, particularly in women of reproductive years. SAD sufferers report symptoms that range from fatigue, depression and anxiety to sleep problems and loss of libido.

The amount of light that enters our eyes stimulates nerve centres in the brain that control mood and set our body clocks. When it is dark the pineal gland produces melatonin, a hormone that makes us sleepy. Bright light, on the other hand, halts the production of melatonin and instead stimulates the production of the 'happy' hormone serotonin. Everyone is naturally more lethargic on gloomy days, but SAD sufferers seem to suffer from a more acute loss of serotonin than is usual for other people.

Various remedies have been recommended, but the most effective is light therapy. Sometimes a daylight-simulation bulb will provide the boost of light levels required. Other devices include light boxes, which deliver 10,000 lux, equivalent to bright morning light, light visors (worn like baseball caps) and lights that gradually brighten in a simulation of dawn.

Opposite: *Different areas in the home require different levels of light, according to the type of activities that take place there. Bedrooms and bathrooms do not need to be as brightly lit as kitchens and studies, where concentrated work is carried out.*

Assessing

Light levels and interior surfaces

Light levels are profoundly affected by interior surfaces and finishes. Light travels through space and bounces off each surface it meets. When it hits a surface, a proportion of that light is absorbed and the rest is reflected. Smooth, light, glossy surfaces are the most reflective, while matt, dark and textured surfaces are the least reflective. Put simply, that means you will need fewer light sources and lower wattage to achieve the same lux levels in a room where the walls, ceiling and floor are white than you would in the same room if it were decorated in dark colours and materials.

A related issue is the direction of light. Any highly directional light, such as a downlight with a narrow beam, will create an intense pool of light that will be brighter the closer it is to the source. Background light diffused over the planes of walls and ceiling will have a lower overall level because some of the light will have been absorbed by each of the surfaces it meets.

Opposite: *Dark matt surfaces are very light-absorbent. This dramatic bathroom, clad in black tile, is soothing rather than oppressive, elegant rather than Gothic. The white interior of the bathtub and niche provide graphic contrast, while candlelight adds to the air of mystery.*

Above: *All-white décor makes the most of available light and is inherently space-enhancing. Limestone, mosaic tile, mirror and frosted glass are all light-reflective surfaces that create a mood of tranquillity.*

Left: Low-voltage halogen spots mounted on the underside of wall units provide discreet kitchen lighting and are not as inefficient in power usage as tungsten equivalents.
Opposite: One way to save energy is to make the most of whatever natural light each room receives in order to reduce dependence on artificial sources during the daytime. Translucent rather than opaque window treatments, glass screens and dividers and light-toned decoration are all ways of enhancing natural light.

Lighting and energy consumption

Artificial lighting accounts for about 10 per cent of the amount of energy consumed by the average household. You can save both money and energy by replacing ordinary bulbs with bulbs that are energy-efficient. The standard domestic light bulb is the tungsten bulb, which converts a mere 5 per cent of the electricity it uses into light. The rest is emitted as heat, which is why these bulbs are so hot to touch. Compact fluorescent bulbs use 75 per cent less electricity, produce six times as much light as tungsten bulbs – which means you can use lower wattages – and last ten times longer. Over its life span, a compact fluorescent bulb prevents half a tonne of carbon dioxide from entering the atmosphere.

However, it is certainly true that the light emitted by compact fluorescents is still not as attractive as the light from either tungsten or halogen bulbs. Tungsten, the light source with which we are most familiar, is inherently warm and intimate; halogen is white and clean-looking. Fluorescent lamps are improving all the time, but they still have a slight greenish cast that is not particularly hospitable. You can warm up the light by using it in conjunction with a tinted shade; if you do not want to use these bulbs in main living areas, at least adopt them in more utilitarian contexts where you will not be so bothered by shortfalls in atmosphere.

More passively, you can reduce dependence on artificial lighting by ensuring that you make the most of whatever natural light a room receives. See page 56 for 'Working with natural light'. Other strategies include putting lights on dimmers. Dimmed tungsten and halogen bulbs last longer because they consume less power, which means that you also save money by not having to replace bulbs as frequently. Similarly, putting external lighting on sensors, so that the light is on only when you need it, both reduces energy consumption and light pollution. See page 181 for other energy-saving tips.

Opposite: *Lighting should be considered early on in the design process so that it works with architectural features, décor and the quality of natural light. Recessed downlights, reflected in an antique mirror, light a kitchen counter, while strip lights positioned under shelves highlight a decorative display.*

Assessment checklist

● How much natural light does the room or area receive? Simple window treatments, such as blinds that pull up well clear of the window or shutters that can be folded back away from the frame, maximize the amount of natural light in the interior. Strategically placed mirrors or glazed partitions can also help to spread light around, particularly to fully internal areas such as corridors, halls, stairs and landings.

● Which direction does/do the window/windows face? In the northern hemisphere rooms that face south are warmer and sunnier than those that face north, where the light is whiter and cooler. Northlight is favoured by artists because it renders colours more faithfully and is more even and shadow-free, but it is not as hospitable and comfortable for living areas where the prime activity is relaxing.

● Which areas in the room are underlit? Which are overlit? Is there a central fixture which may be causing glare?

● Think about architectural and spatial quality. Is the room high-ceilinged and spacious or is it confined? Are there details or features to which you might wish to draw attention?

● Think about decoration. Would a different scheme better enhance the overall quality of light? You might consider, for example, replacing dark carpeting with light-toned wood flooring in a room that receives poor natural light.

● Think about patterns of circulation, or how you move about the room during the course of the day. Are there enough switches so that you can easily control lights both individually and by the main entrance to the room?

● Think about which activities take place in the room. Does your existing lighting arrangement provide enough flexibility to support all those different functions? Would dimmer switches further increase your options?

● Consider whether there is any risk that water or steam might come in contact with light fittings. This may well be the case in kitchens, and will almost certainly be true in most bathrooms and shower rooms. Specially sealed fittings and bulbs are required for these areas.

● How recently has your wiring been updated? Electrical systems that are between 15 and 20 years old normally require upgrading. Signs of deteriorating wiring include fuses that blow frequently for no good reason, cables whose external sheathing or insulation have become brittle and worn away and old-fashioned sockets or switches. Rewiring is unavoidably disruptive because cabling must be channelled within walls and under floors, which entails subsequent replastering, redecorating and sometimes reflooring. At the same time, it can provide an opportunity to improve the basic electrical infrastructure by repositioning sockets, adding new sockets and switches or installing fixed forms of lighting such as track lights and downlights.

In some countries, such as the UK, there is no law that says you cannot carry out domestic electrical work yourself, but don't even think about it unless you have the relevant skills and experience. Always err on the safe side and consult an accredited professional, preferably one who comes with a personal recommendation or references. In some parts of the world, notably Germany, all electrical work – including wiring plugs – must be handled by professionals.

Types of lighting

Before going on to consider your choice of light fittings and light sources, it is important to gain a basic appreciation of the main types of lighting and what purposes they serve. Occasionally, specific fittings fall squarely into a certain category; more commonly there is a degree of overlap, depending on how you make use of a particular light. An anglepoise, for example, is a good example of a directional or 'task' light and was designed specifically for desk work. However, angled so that light shines upwards, reflecting off the ceiling or a wall, an anglepoise can also function as a very effective background light.

Diffused or background light

Background light is – or should be – the most discreet form of artificial lighting. Depending on how it is delivered, you may not notice the light fitting at all, merely its glowing effect on walls, ceilings and other surfaces such as table tops and floors. Some form of diffusion is essential, either by simply shielding the light source with a shade or by bouncing light off reflective planes. A series of shaded table lamps situated at key points around the room can serve as background lighting; so, too, can a combination of uplighters, downlights, wall-washers, side lights, track lighting and even directional lighting angled towards a wall or ceiling.

In practical terms, background light provides the most obvious replacement for natural light when levels are low or in hours of darkness; as such, it is required in almost every area in the home. Aesthetically, good background lighting can go a long way to generate mood and atmosphere by accentuating spatial quality, enhancing volume and creating overlapping pools of light and shade. On the other hand, where there is too great a reliance on a single central light – such as a bright pendant, for example – a room may be adequately lit for practical purposes but is likely to be devoid of character and interest. That doesn't matter if the room in question is where you do the laundry, but it is a severe drawback in a living area or any other part of the home where creating a mood of relaxation is important. Because background light is often called upon to supplement natural light levels, dimmer controls can be invaluable.

Information light

This type of lighting is required only in specific areas of the home, where there is a need for a small amount of local light for orientation, to facilitate a task or to illuminate a dark corner. Fridge and oven lights are good example of information light; so are lights in cupboards or closets that are triggered by the opening of a door, as well as external lights over doorbells or keyholes or along pathways. Although information light is fairly mundane and practical by definition, low level lights recessed into skirting boards (baseboards) or along stairs provide an example of a more evocative application.

Directional light

As the term suggests, directional light delivers a focused narrowish beam to a specific area, either to provide a boost of light to enable close work to be carried out, or to accentuate a particular feature or display. There are a huge range of fittings which serve this function, from desk lights of various descriptions to spotlights and picture lights.

Desk lights, spotlights and track fittings are generally adjustable so that you can target light right where you need it

Opposite: *Information light, which tends to be very specific and local, is chiefly practical in effect. However, this does not mean it has to be banal.*

This built-in bathroom storage, which is lit internally, performs its function perfectly well, but equally it is as attractive as any decorative display.

Above: *Background light should be discreet and diffused so the light source is not visible at all. Here, lights concealed behind a headboard wash the wall with a soft, peaceful glow. Low-level light sources are more comfortable in bedrooms than lights shining down from above.*

Left: Directional or focused light is particularly important in the kitchen. Here, clusters of four ceiling-mounted spots train light at the preparation areas. Light must be targeted so that it shines directly on work surfaces or reflects off walls, which means positioning fittings close to the wall. Any further back and you run the risk of working in your own shadow.

Opposite: Decorative light adds a playful touch to the interior. Examples here include Tom Dixon's 'Jack' light, a chandelier lit by candles and a table lamp with a pierced metal shade. None of these light sources contributes much in the way of overall illumination, but their charm and appeal is undeniable.

by angling the fitting itself. Recessed downlights, however, do not always provide this degree of flexibility, which means particular care must be taken over their installation. Many directional lights have fairly deep shades or cowls, both to prevent the sideways spill or diffusion of light and to reduce glare. The closer they are placed to the area in question the brighter the light will be.

Strip lights can also serve as directional lights if they are concealed. Lights mounted beneath kitchen wall units, for example, provide task light for counters and worktops; strip lights hidden behind upstands accent shelving or display cases. The linearity of such effects can be exploited to highlight architectural detail and to make built-in features or large pieces of furniture appear to 'float'.

Decorative light

In recent years, there has been an upsurge of interest in what might be called decorative light, which embraces a wide variety of playful, sculptural and innovative designs that serve little practical function but offer immense charm and delight. Many decorative lights do not add much in the way of illumination – indeed, their light output may be quite low – but they make a beguiling addition to any lighting scheme. From the ubiquitous string of fairy lights or the retro classic lava lamp, to lit sculptures such as Tom Dixon's 'Jack' light or Ingo Maurer's 'Bird', the popularity of decorative light is evidence of our enduring fascination with lighting effects.

In this category might also be included firelight and candlelight, those warm, hospitable and evocative light sources that stubbornly continue to be present in our homes long after technology has superseded any practical benefits they might deliver.

Specific requirements

Most areas in the home, excluding perhaps the most utilitarian such as a laundry room, for which a single overhead light will suffice, require a variety of different types of light, so daily routines and activities can be carried out there safely and effectively. At the same time, it is also important to consider comfort levels and overall mood and atmosphere.

As a starting point, think about the most important and frequent activity you perform in any given room or area, then consider any other additional functions the space must fulfil from time to time. A living area, for example, may be used on a daily basis in the evening for watching television or listening to music, but it may also often double up as a place for study or music practice or a hobby such as needlework, and more occasionally as the venue for parties and celebrations.

As well as practical constraints, you will also want to devote a little thought to the particular mood you are trying to create. Rooms where the emphasis is on relaxation will need gentler, softer lighting than working areas such as kitchens, which require more robust treatment.

Front entrances

Safety and security are prime concerns for external lighting, most particularly any lighting that illuminates the route from pavement or driveway to the front door itself.
• Light steps, paths, drives and porches adequately with low-level external fittings, particularly if you live in a country area where there is no street lighting.
• Make sure there is a light by the side of or above the front door so the house number or name can be easily read by someone driving past in the street.
• Light the garage or any side-gate entrances.
• An information light is useful beside a doorbell or lock.
• External fittings should be robust and weatherproof, and well-diffused to prevent glare.
• Choose low-energy bulbs for efficiency and economy or put lights on switches that are triggered by movement or heat.
• Powerful 'approach' lighting is a known deterrent to crime.
• Avoid glare, which may dazzle motorists or pedestrians and cause accidents. Make sure lights are bright enough to be informative but not overbright.

Halls

Whether it is a mere threshold, or a room in its own right, the entrance hall is a place of transition between the outside world and the privacy of your home. Lighting should be warm and welcoming, but not so bright that your eyes have to work hard to adjust to differing light levels, either when coming in from outdoors or when leaving the house.
• Fixed or recessed light fittings make sense in hallways, particularly narrow ones, as you do not need to take into account the possibility of future furniture rearrangement.
• Pendants, lanterns or chandeliers add decorative interest in an area that is often minimally furnished and can provide a central focus that accentuates the welcoming aspect.
• Side lights or uplights will generate an expansive feeling and give a soft, diffused, glare-free light.
• If the hall is generously proportioned, you can include table or standing lamps, provided the flexes are kept well out of the way of the main traffic routes.
• Position a light switch right by the front door in the most obvious position so you don't have to fumble in the dark.

Opposite: *Strip lighting provides an intriguing way of lighting an entrance hall, giving even illumination while highlighting the architecture.*

Above: *Wall-mounted fittings are a practical solution for lighting stairs and landings. This decorative branched fitting provides gentle background light.*

Left: *A minimal stairway is edge-lit with concealed lighting, enhancing the clean lines of the architectural detailing without detracting from the purity of the blank walls.*

Opposite: *A contemporary version of the chandelier, with its long teardrops of glass, provides a welcome focus of interest on a landing. Central fixtures, which may be intrusive elsewhere, are very effective in halls, landings and entrances.*

Stairs

It is often best to plan stair lighting in tandem with hall lighting, coordinating fittings for a more considered effect.

• Make sure there are switches at the top and bottom of the stairs and at intermediate levels or landings.

• Stairs must be evenly lit to prevent accidents – moody effects of light and shade can be hazardous.

• Side lighting makes obvious sense on stairways; omni-directional pendant fixtures are also practical.

• Low-level lights recessed behind skirting boards (baseboards) or in stair treads have a modern architectural edge.

Kitchens

In the contemporary home, the kitchen is increasingly an all-purpose area. While it may be chiefly defined by its working role, it has also become much more of a sociable space, where family and friends gather. Overall lighting levels should be relatively high – two to three times what you would require in a living room – in order for kitchen tasks to be carried out safely and efficiently. At the same time, it is also important to build in flexibility for creating more atmospheric effects when entertaining or relaxing over a meal.

• Whether your kitchen is fully fitted, freestanding or a mixture of the two, the positions of sink, oven and hob are likely to be fixed by existing servicing arrangements. For this reason, fixed or fitted forms of lighting, such as downlights and track lights, can make good sense in a kitchen. You can be fairly confident that the basic layout will remain unchanged in the future, so this will allow you to target working areas in the expectation that they will remain in the same places.

• Try to avoid having central pendants or ceiling lights for background lighting because these cast obscuring shadows into the corners of the room. Wall-mounted uplights are a much better solution, as are strip lights mounted at the top of wall units that wash the ceiling with light.

• Don't use freestanding lights or table lamps anywhere in the kitchen. They clutter up kitchen work surfaces, require sockets that might be better employed for appliances and have trailing flexes that can present a safety hazard.

• Glare can be just as hazardous as low light. Ensure that light levels are as even as possible. Directional lights, such as spotlights, should be positioned so that you are not working in your own shadow, which generally means placing them to the front or side of where you will be working. Strip lights mounted on the underside of wall units are a highly effective way of lighting counters and worktops.

• Think about future maintenance. Avoid fussy fittings that might be difficult to clean in the event of a build-up of grease. Recessed fittings are the neatest and least obtrusive.

• Reflective surfaces such as stainless steel, tile and glass can multiply the overall amount of light in a room – but guard against the possibility of an irritating glare being set up by light bouncing at particular angles.

• Information lighting is usefully incorporated in ventilation hoods and within deep larder cupboards.

• Dimmable lights allow you to vary the mood if the kitchen doubles up as an eating area, especially for evening dining.

Eating areas

Whether you eat in the kitchen, in a separate dining room, or within a multipurpose open-plan living space, the focus of attention is the table. All meals are not the same, however, and you need to incorporate sufficient flexibility to cater for different moods, occasions and times of day.

• Keep light levels soft and subtle, but not so dim that you can't actually see what's on your plate.

• Pendant fittings create a cosy focus. They should be hung low enough to avoid irritating glare, but not so low that they interfere with views across the table.

• Side lighting, such as wall-mounted sconces or uplights, provides a good source of background light and prevents the eating area from feeling too enclosed. The same effect can be gained by using table or standing lamps, provided they are positioned away from the table itself.

• Downlights are not ideal in eating areas, as it can be difficult to judge positioning to avoid harsh glare.

• Accent any pictures or decorative displays in the room to provide background interest.

• Dimmer switches are invaluable for eating areas. They allow you to control the light levels instantly according to the time of day and the particular occasion.

Top left: *A well-lit interior will always include many different sources of light, some of which are directional and focused and some of which are more diffused. Here, a pair of downlights recessed in the ceiling illuminate a dining table; niches are lit to provide a soft background glow and brighter task light picks out the working area of the kitchen counter.*

Centre left: *Many ventilation hoods incorporate built-in lights to illuminate hobs. Track lighting, which allows you to position lights where you want them, are also useful in kitchen lighting schemes.*

Below left: *Kitchen lighting requires careful planning. Here, undershelf light specifically directed at the worktop is combined with small glass pendants for background illumination. Fairy lights draped around a wall-hung display cabinet add a light-hearted decorative touch.*

Opposite: *A backlit wall provides softly glowing background light for an eating area in the kitchen. The table is lit with two overscaled 'Icon' pendants, designed by Ferruccio Laviani for Kartell. The red plastic shades, which prevent the light from being too glaring, have Pop Art appeal.*

Living rooms and multipurpose areas

What goes on in your living room? Very probably, many different activities, some of them sociable in nature, others more solitary or work-related. For most families, the living room is the multimedia centre, the home of audio and visual equipment such as the television and music system. At the same time, it may incorporate an eating area – perhaps a kitchen as well if your home is open-plan – along with an area devoted to working. Perhaps your home computer is sited in the living room to give easy and open access for all the family. Then again, living rooms tend to be places where we are more likely to entertain our family and friends and, as a consequence, we are generally prepared to go to more effort and expense in our attempts to make them attractive and welcoming. Lighting plays a huge role both in reconciling the very different requirements of a multipurpose space and in expressing a sense of our personal style.

• Chandeliers and other central fixtures remain popular in living rooms because they provide a focus. The secret of using such fixtures successfully is not to rely on them for the sole source of illumination. The greater proportion of background lighting should be coming from other sources – uplights, table and standing lamps and wall lights, for example – which then allows you to use bulbs of low wattage in a central light and avoid the harsh and rather deadening effect that results when a central light is too bright.

• The average living room – and any other space of equivalent size – needs between four and five different light sources to be comfortably and atmospherically lit.

• Uplights will accentuate any architectural detailing, such as cornicing and mouldings, and can make a room feel more spacious and high-ceilinged if the ceiling is pale in colour.

• Avoid using downlights in living areas. To be really effective, downlighting must be positioned according to the furniture layout, and this can then restrict your options for future rearrangement once the fittings are installed.

• Vary the heights at which lights are positioned. Even if you are going to be sitting most of the time when you are in the living room, remember to include lights that are both higher up and lower down than this level to bring a greater degree of animation and vitality to the overall effect.

• Living areas often benefit from an infrastructure of multiple lighting circuits – a minimum of at least two. This gives you greater flexibility and control. Table lamps can be wired so that they can be controlled both individually and by a master switch positioned at the entrance of the room.

• Highlight decorative displays and pictures with spotlights, picture lights or strip lights concealed behind baffles.

• For reading or other concentrated work, you will need directional light focused on the page or desktop, from a light that can be angled and adjusted according to need.

• Include a light beside or behind the television to avoid eyestrain. Remember that the television screen itself emits light, so it is important to make sure that there is not too great a contrast between it and the rest of the room.

• Don't forget to put lights on dimmer switches so that you can vary mood and atmosphere when you need to.

• Light that is purely decorative is especially entrancing in a living room where it can be appreciated by everyone.

Opposite: *'Hanging Pods', designed by Margaret O'Rorke, are thrown porcelain forms suspended from a low-voltage system.*

Above: *Delightfully bristly, these 'Eight-Fifty' pendant lights by Claire Norcross are made from the plastic tags used in industrial packaging and are hung over a table to define a dining area within an open-plan room.*

Right: *Living rooms need light sources at different heights. One of the easiest ways of achieving this is to use table and floor lamps, judiciously positioned around the room.*

Studies and work rooms

Most work carried out in the home that is unrelated to household routines and maintenance involves reading, writing and computer use: in other words, it is desk-based.

• For any form of concentrated work, you need to boost light levels significantly – which means you will need between three and five times the level of light you would provide in a living area or bedroom. This light must be targeted at the focus of attention, whether it is the keyboard or the page.

• Be sure to provide adequate levels of background light, too, otherwise there will be too great a contrast between the immediate working area and the rest of the room.

• Uplighting is the best form of background light for computer work since it avoids reflections or shadows on the screen.

• Directional task light is essential. Adjustable desk lights should be positioned to one side so that they shine on the page or keyboard. Fittings with deep shades or cowls mean there is no risk of glare from the bulb itself.

Bedrooms

The bedroom is the ultimate personal retreat and requires sensitive lighting to allow for the shift of natural light conditions between night and day. In the evening, soft, ambient light promotes relaxation; in the morning, brighter, more cheerful light helps you to face the day.

• Avoid overhead fixtures. They produce relatively harsh light and can cause glare when viewed from a prone position.

• Background lighting can be delivered by a combination of bedside lamps, wall lights and uplights.

• For reading in bed, wall lights or bedside lights that can be repositioned and adjusted are useful.

• Make sure you can control all lights from the bedroom door and from the bedside. Dimmer switches allow you to respond to different moods and natural light conditions.

• Information lights, triggered by the opening of a wardrobe or closet door, aid clothes selection.

• In children's rooms, try to avoid any freestanding lights with flexes that can be tugged and pulled over or present a tripping hazard. Cover sockets with socket protectors.

• Young children are often afraid of the dark or may wake at night and need to find their way to the bathroom safely. Nightlights that emit a low glow will not disturb sleeping patterns but can be a welcome source of reassurance and security.

Above: *Concentrated work, such as drawing, requires a high level of illumination and as much natural light as possible. Here, a drawing board set up on a mezzanine level benefits from the daylight spilling in from the expanse of window. Spotlights recessed in the sloping ceiling planes provide background light, while an adjustable task light gives a boost of targeted illumination.*

Opposite: *Computer screens are light sources in themselves and care must be taken not to cause distracting reflections on the screen. The best form of background light is some form of uplighting; you will also need task light directed at the keyboard.*

Opposite left: *Concealed or recessed lighting is ideal for use in the bathroom. Here, both sink and storage areas are fitted with fixed lights to provide even illumination. Make sure the fittings you choose are approved for bathroom use.*

Opposite right: *As in kitchens, wall-hung bathroom units or cabinets offer the opportunity to conceal lighting below or above. In this case, a pair of strip lights have been fitted to the underside of the cabinets to impart a diffusing glow.*

Above: *A purely decorative feature takes the place of a central light in this elegant bedroom. The background lighting is supplied by lights concealed behind the headboard, with the addition of small table lamps for reading in bed.*

Right: *If you do want to use a pendant or ceiling fixture in the bedroom, make sure it is not too bright and that it is balanced by other light sources. Here, a pendant hung low with the bulb well shaded provides soft background light.*

Bathrooms

Even if your bathroom is not a fully fledged wet room with a shower draining directly to the floor, it is still by far the wettest room in the home. Water and electricity are lethal in combination, so safety is a prime consideration. At the same time, harsh or utilitarian bathroom lighting can stand in the way of relaxation. It is worth making the effort to light the bathroom with as much attention to character and ambience as you would apply to more obvious living areas so that you can enjoy the time you spend there.

• Bathroom light fittings must be fully enclosed and approved for use in damp environments. There should be no means by which steam or water could come in contact with the bulb and all metal parts must also be sealed.

• In Britain, switches must either be the pull-cord type or positioned outside the bathroom door. In the United States, where switches are grounded, normal switches can be used.

• Avoid using table or standing lamps, pendants or adjustable spotlights.

• Recessed and fixed lights, such as wall lights and downlights, are ideal for bathroom use.

• Supplement background lighting with side lights flanking the mirror for putting on make-up and shaving. You can also obtain bathroom mirrors and cabinets with integral lights.

• Fibre optics – where the light source is positioned remotely from the points at which light is emitted – is a glamorous and atmospheric way of lighting showerheads and tubs.

Gardens

Garden lighting can be impromptu and temporary – such as flares and nightlights strategically positioned for a summer party or barbecue – or it can be a more permanent installation that transforms the garden after dark into an outdoor room and source of visual delight.

• All external electrical lighting and cabling must be installed by a qualified professional.

• Fittings must be fully weatherproof, approved for exterior use and kept clear of debris.

• Cabling should be buried so there is no risk of accidental damage (and electrocution) when using lawnmowers and other garden tools.

• External circuits must incorporate a circuit-breaker and should be controllable indoors.

• Guard against overlighting, which is a nuisance for neighbours and contributes to light pollution. Dim lights, positioned at low level, accent planting, trees and water features without flooding the immediate vicinity with unacceptably high levels of light.

Above left: *Festive garden lighting: shaded candles transform a driveway into a ceremonial route, while strings of bulbs looped around trees and bushes add to the magical effect.*

Above: Garden lighting is often most effective when it is low level, positioned to highlight foliage and branches. This type of arrangement is also less intrusive for neighbours.
Left: Bouncing light off a plain surface, such as a garden wall, can create enough background light for enjoying evenings outdoors.

Designing a lighting scheme

With a little preparation, you can design your own lighting scheme using the guidelines set out in this section. If, however, you find it difficult to decide which options are the best for your particular requirements, you can always commission a professional designer. Some large lighting companies have showrooms with full blackout facilities, which enable you to view demonstrations of different specific effects. Other lighting suppliers and consultants provide a design and advisory service for a small fee. All you have to supply is a sketch plan of the room or rooms in question, and perhaps a few photographs, and a lighting designer will be able to come up with an original design and lighting plan to meet your needs.

It is always a good idea to pay a visit to a lighting showroom or supplier before embarking on the design process. Lighting is one area of design that has seen significant technological changes in recent years and new types of fitting are coming onto the market all the time. If you investigate what's available beforehand, you are more likely to come up with a scheme that exploits the potential of this exciting element to the full.

Make a plan

Whether you decide to go it alone or intend to consult a professional designer, the first step is to make a sketch of the room or area, making a note of existing permanent features, including fireplaces, windows, doors, recesses and radiators, along with the current electrical

Left: *Spotlights fitted on the underside of a ventilation unit provide targeted light for a kitchen island in this converted loft. Strip lighting concealed between two halves of fitted storage bathes the stairway in an atmospheric blue glow.*
Opposite: *For the best results, you should try to consider lighting early on in the design process. Here, a number of recessed downlights have been carefully positioned to light the kitchen and dining areas and to bring out architectural detail.*

scheme

Experiment

Before you commit yourself to a new lighting infrastructure, or venture out to buy a range of fittings, you can experiment to gauge the effect of different types of light. Equip yourself with a ladder, a couple of extension leads, car inspection lamps, clip-on spotlights or small table lamps, along with bulbs of different wattages. Pans, colanders or tin foil that you can use as reflectors or diffusers also come in useful. Enlist the help of a couple of friends or family members so you can assess the effect of multiple light sources.

First of all, try out lights in parts of the room that are presently underlit to gauge the effect. You may be surprised how different a room appears when you have added lights in otherwise dark corners. Try out different combinations of wattages. If you are increasing the number of light sources in an area, you can afford to use bulbs of lower wattage: the combined effect will be just as bright but more atmospheric. Check your present lighting infrastructure to see if you have the necessary sockets to support your requirements.

The second aspect to consider is the direction of light. If the area in question has an overhead fitting, turn it off and try to achieve the same overall level of brightness by shining light upwards to reflect off the ceiling or sideways to bounce off the walls. Think carefully about positioning. The effect of uplighting is lost if the fitting is placed too high up the wall and close to the ceiling. Varying where lights are positioned on the vertical plane – lower down, midway and higher up – has more vitality than positioning them all at the same level.

Installation

However much or little professional assistance you have had during the design process, installation should be a matter for a qualified electrician. Of course, you don't need to comb the Yellow Pages if all you intend to do is plug in a few new table lamps. Anything else – which includes rewiring, installing downlights and other types of fixed or recessed fittings, adding new sockets and switches and installing external lighting – is best not tackled by amateurs.

You may also wish to consult an electrician in advance of buying new lighting to check that what you are planning is feasible. Recessed forms of lighting, for example, require a sufficient ceiling void so that they are adequately ventilated, which can rule them out in older properties.

arrangements, such as the position of sockets, switches and ceiling fixtures. You should also mark on the plan any built-in features such as shelving or cupboards, as well as the position of large, bulky items of furniture – for example, sofas and beds – that you do not foresee rearranging at any future date.

The next step is to take accurate measurements and make a scale plan, transferring your sketch to graph paper. This will help you to assess your particular requirements or can form the basis of a subsequent dialogue with a professional, either a designer, if you choose to take that route, or the electrician who will implement your ideas. Think about where light levels are currently less than adequate and mark any dark areas on the plan. You should also consider whether there are enough switches and sockets for your needs and whether it might be beneficial to have an additional lighting circuit installed, so you can control background light and local light independently.

If you find it difficult to assess present lighting conditions with the naked eye, you could always try using a camera. This method is excellent for giving you a clear, accurate indication of where lighting is poor, and the photographs themselves are invaluable for reference. Take photos of the room under different lighting conditions, both during the day and in the evening, to see where additional light may be needed or where current lighting arrangements may be causing glare.

Opposite: *In a very effective combination of natural light, intimate focused light and task light, a pendant fitting is looped across to hang low* *over a dining table set under a skylight, while downlights, positioned very close to the wall, direct light at the working area of the kitchen.*

Above: *Downlights make good sense in kitchens and other fitted areas where layout and arrangement tend to be fixed for a good long time.* *Here, downlights recessed in the ceiling are used to light a kitchen counter, as well as a sink and hob that are set in separate alcoves.*

Case study

An interior at different times of the day

Spatial quality is intimately bound up with light. This three-storey Victorian terraced house, the home of a designer and an architect, has been transformed from the typical dark warren of small enclosed rooms into a series of bright and airy spaces that provide an easy and uplifting backdrop to modern living. Lighting considerations, in terms of both natural and artificial light, were integral to the entire design process, informing decisions about structural alterations every bit as much as the decorative choices.

From the outset, the couple knew that they wanted to make the house as light as possible. In terraced houses, however, natural light enters only at the front and the rear, leaving the central core of the house dark. In basic structural terms, two principal strategies were adopted to improve daylighting. Firstly, the spaces on the ground floor were opened up to produce long vistas to the south-facing garden and, secondly, a rooflight was installed above the stairs to draw natural light down into the upper storeys.

On the ground level, partitions were removed to create an open-plan layout running from the dining area at the front, facing the street, through a seating area to the kitchen at the rear of the house, which gives onto the garden. Large expanses of glass, front and rear, make the most of available natural light, while a glazed door extends the view from the

Above left: *In the main seating area, blue ambient light spills out from behind the false ceiling.*
Opposite: *The ground floor is an open sweep of space with long vistas right through to the south-facing garden. On the dining-area side of the false ceiling, the ambient lighting is a warm purplish shade.*
Following pages: *Carefully positioned downlights bounce light from walls and pick out individual pictures and objects (left). With the downlights switched off, the coloured lighting gains in intensity, reflected off pure white walls and ceiling (right).*

Above: A rooflight positioned over the top of the stairway spills light down through the top two storeys of the house through a glazed landing floor. Open treads allow the low angles of winter light to penetrate into the interior. The glazed panel screening the bathroom from the lower landing reads like a light box when the bathroom lights are on.

Right: The shower room on the top floor is enclosed with translucent screens of sandblasted glass to let the light stream through.

Above: The downlights used throughout the house can be pivoted at will so that light can be directed to pick out different objects and pictures in a tight focus of attention.

Right: The key to using downlights successfully is not to position them so that the light falls in the centre of the room, where it will be wasted, but to place them about 450–600mm (14–20in) from the wall so that the light can be bounced off the surface. Here, fitted storage painted white serves as a good reflective plane.

seating area through to the garden. Had the house been wider, the couple might have considered employing different finishes on the walls and floor. As it is relatively narrow, they decided to keep the decoration as light as possible to enhance the sense of space. Accordingly, the walls, ceilings and woodwork are painted a warm white that takes the chill off winter light and dazzles in the summer. The flooring is light-toned French oak.

Without some hint of definition between different areas of activity, open-plan layouts can run the risk of becoming amorphous spaces. Rather than interrupt the clear sweep of space, the ingenious solution was to create a false ceiling marking the transition between the seating and the dining areas. Concealed behind the false ceiling are fluorescent tubes wrapped in coloured photo film so the ambient light is blue on the seating-area side and a warmer purplish colour on the dining-area side. Carefully positioned downlights in the living area are focused to pick out some of the photographs and other objects on display. The downlights here and in the rest of the house have integral black baffles that recess the lights further into the ceiling so that there is no risk of glare.

In the kitchen, similar strategies were employed. Downlights are positioned directly above the worktop so that there is no risk of obscuring shadows. The counter itself is made of 'Arena' stone, a pale Italian composite of light granite and limestone that is very durable, stain- and heat-resistant and does not require the demanding maintenance of stainless steel. A warm fluorescent tube mounted behind the frosted-glass splashback creates a spectacular effect at night. While many types of glass have a greenish tinge, this splashback is made of opalite white glass that gives a purer light when backlit.

The large windows and sliding glazed door make the most of the south-facing aspect. Leading the eye onwards, the kitchen counter and units are extended outdoors down one side of the garden, coincidentally providing a useful storage space for garden tools and the children's bikes and toys. When an outdoor space reads as an extension of the interior, this type of strategy offers an important way of reducing visual clutter. Similarly, care was taken to ensure that the levels, indoors and out, were absolutely flush. The timber flooring of the interior extends to hardwood timber decking outdoors, which has a very calming effect. At the side of the house, a flower bed planted with black bamboo is uplit, which enhances the view through the glazed door in the seating area.

On the upper levels, the skylight, in combination with the clever use of glazed panels, draws sunlight into the heart of the house. Positioned directly over the stairs, the skylight sends light streaming right down to the first floor where the bedrooms are located, through a glass floor on the landing. Rather than use expensive toughened glass, the glass for the landing floor consists of a layer of laminated glass bonded to a reflective aluminium waffle layer. Open treads on the stairs to the second floor allow the low angles of winter sun to penetrate into the house. The second-floor shower room and first-floor bathroom are both enclosed with panels and screens of sandblasted glass, letting natural light through during the daytime. At night, interior illumination transforms the spaces into glowing light boxes. Finely judged effects of both natural and artificial light animate the entire interior at every level. As this particular example shows, there is a strong case to be made for putting lighting at the very centre of your design and decorative decisions.

Above, left to right: *The kitchen under different lighting conditions. During the day, natural light spills in through large glazed openings and is reflected off light-toned surfaces and finishes (opposite left). In the early evening, downlights light the preparation area (opposite right). As it grows darker, the backlit splashback provides an additional burst of illumination (above left). With the downlights switched off, the splashback gives off a gentle glow that silhouettes objects on the counter (above right).*

designing

'Architecture', as Le Corbusier wrote, is 'the masterly, correct and magnificent play of volumes brought together in light.' Light gives space presence. It describes volume, reveals form and creates an animating progression from area to area. When you design with light, you literally manipulate and enhance your perception of your surroundings, bringing certain features to the fore and suppressing others that are less welcome, in order to achieve maximum character and depth.

with light

Working with natural light

Many of us spend the greatest proportion of our week working or living in artificially lit conditions. It may only be during our lunch breaks or at weekends that we spend more than a few minutes outdoors in daylight. For this reason, it can be difficult for us to appreciate how profoundly we are affected by natural light. In our grandmothers' day, babies were often wheeled into the garden in their prams on fine afternoons for a little fresh air and sunshine. This practice might smack of neglect today, and it has certainly all but disappeared, but recent research indicates that previous generations might have instinctively appreciated something we now overlook. New studies have revealed that babies who are exposed to an extra boost of sunshine during the day sleep better at night because of the effect natural light has on their circadian rhythms.

Natural light sets our body clocks. The stimulus of dawn light controls a pacemaker in the brain, which in turn delivers the right hormones at the right time, so making us active during the day and sleepy at night. Centuries ago, when artificial means of lighting meant expensive candles and most of the population laboured outdoors, people rose with the sun and went to bed when it got dark. Few of us would accept such patterns today or could operate productively within such limits. Yet, despite the fact that our lives have grown progressively orientated towards the indoors, we remain no less attuned, biologically speaking, to those natural rhythms. It's not just the fresh air and exercise that sees us yawning after a long country walk and heading off for an early night, it's the prolonged exposure to full-spectrum daylight. Similarly, many insomniacs report that their sleeping disorders began following a major disruption such as a period of stress or illness that kept them awake on successive nights, or the jet lag suffered after a long-haul flight.

As outlined in the previous section, daylight is incredibly bright when compared to artificial lighting. Even on a grey, overcast day – the sort that most of us moan about as being dark and gloomy – daylight is still three times brighter than the light levels in the average living room. Bright sunshine, which everyone naturally experiences as uplifting, is 100 times brighter than that. In addition, the light levels at dawn, which set our body clocks, are 50 times brighter than most office lighting.

And it is not simply a question of degree. Daylight is full-spectrum light, which means that it is equally balanced across all the wavelengths. By contrast, all artificial light is skewed towards one part of the spectrum or another. In the case of the standard domestic light source, the familiar tungsten bulb, that inherent bias creates light that is warm and yellowish, while fluorescent lamps have a greenish cast. Daylight is the only light that gives us true colour representation. You can appreciate this fact very easily if you take a coloured fabric swatch outdoors: the colours will appear quite different, which will be all the more noticeable if the swatch is patterned.

Light levels indoors are never going to approximate outdoor lighting conditions in terms of intensity – and it would feel very uncomfortable if they did. However, we can improve matters considerably through decorative and design choices. Making the most of natural light in our interiors not only keeps us healthy and positive in outlook, it is also kinder to the environment and to our wallets, because it reduces our increasing dependence on energy-consuming artificial sources.

Opposite: *We are incredibly sensitive to the quality of natural light, particularly first thing in the morning. The stimulus of dawn light helps to set our body clocks and keep us in regular sleeping patterns. Slatted blinds provide variable light control; half-open, they create evocative patterns of light and shade.*

natural

Light-enhancing decoration

Most of us today prefer light, spacious surroundings. That was not always the case. In Victorian times, light was treated almost like an unwelcome interloper. Windows were covered with layers of blinds, curtains and drapery so that interiors were shrouded in semi-gloom. While a practical desire to protect furnishing fabrics from the fading caused by bright sunshine might have been one reason behind such a preference, it was more a question of style and taste. A parlour that was dimly lit and had no evident connection with the world outside was a genteel refuge from the prosaic realities of employment. By contrast, a century or so earlier, during the Georgian period, windows were much larger and comparatively minimally screened to allow light into every corner of the interior, expressing the clarity and progress of the age of 'enlightenment' and reason.

Our contemporary desire to live in homes that provide a connection with the outdoors and which are as light-filled as possible owes much to early modernists such as Le Corbusier, who were greatly concerned about the health-giving properties of natural light and fresh air. Flat roofs where people could sunbathe and continuous strip windows were a feature of early modern designs and they coincided with the beginning of the trend to holiday in the sunnier areas of the world. At the same time, developments in technology were allowing for the production of ever greater expanses of glass. Windows were no longer constrained in size to small openings but could fill an entire wall.

The way you decorate and furnish your home can go a long way to maximizing the effect of natural light. Light colours and light-toned surfaces and finishes, such as pale wood, pale stone or tile, and white or off-white paint, reflect more light back into the room, whereas dark colours and highly textured surfaces are more light-absorbent. Any area of the home where you are going

Right: *All-white decoration is serene, reflecting whatever natural light a room receives and enhancing the sense of spaciousness. While such pristine décor is difficult to maintain in areas that see a lot of traffic, it is more practical for bedrooms, where a soothing ambience is welcome.*

to be spending a lot of time during the daylight hours will be much more uplifting if it is decorated in light tones. That's not to say you have to banish strong colour from your home altogether. Even in a working area which is used during the day, colour can be effectively introduced in the form of accents and displays.

Window treatments also have a direct effect on the quality and quantity of natural light that a room receives. Heavy, full curtains with deep headings and drapery or gathered blinds that loop low over the window cut out a significant proportion of light and are best adopted in rooms or areas that will not see much daytime use. Simpler window treatments that can be pulled right back or raised up to reveal the full expanse of the window invite maximum light into the interior, which is a positive asset for working areas such as kitchens and studies. Translucent or semi-transparent curtains or blinds are often a good choice for bedrooms, since they provide privacy while letting the early morning light filter through. Window treatments that are adjustable, such as slatted or Venetian blinds and louvred shutters, allow you to quickly respond to different light conditions and are also an excellent choice in warmer regions of the world where screening out glare and preventing overheating from direct sunshine is much more of an issue.

In the future, glazed walls, windows and their coverings might all serve as 'smart skins', responding to different light levels. In a very recent development, one designer has been experimenting with electroluminescent technology to make a reactive window blind that actually emits light itself, the light increasing in intensity as darkness falls.

Left: *Not everyone wants to live in a fully open-plan space; it can also be useful, and more flexible, to reserve the option to close off an area from time to time, if only to keep sound levels down. Solid partitions, however, can block light unnecessarily. A more flexible solution, as here with the entrance to this large light-filled kitchen, is to opt for glazed partitions and doors that allow light to spread to other areas while still providing a degree of enclosure.*

Borrowing light

In many homes, particularly apartments and terraced houses, there will inevitably be areas that do not receive any direct natural light. In a terraced house, there will be windows solely at the front and the rear of the building; while some apartments will have windows along the front and perhaps one side only. In such circumstances, it is important to make the most of any available light by keeping internal partitions as minimal and transparent as possible, so dark areas benefit from 'borrowed' light.

Fully open-plan layouts, a feature of much contemporary domestic planning, are not only popular because they break down the increasingly redundant barriers between different household activities, but also because they create an illusion of spaciousness by spreading around the available natural light. A common alteration to many Victorian terraces, for example, is to take down the dividing wall between the kitchen and the dining room or between the dining room and the living room. The result is not an increase in floor area per se, but it feels like it, because the new space is lit from the windows both at the front and the rear. In situations where there is a short narrow hallway leading to the stairs it may also be beneficial to remove the partition between the hall and the living area so that the front door opens into an open, inclusive space.

Creating internal windows in partition walls also helps to spread the light around. This type of strategy preserves a feeling of enclosure while allowing slivers or glimpses of views from area to area and aiding natural ventilation. If you do not want a fully open-plan layout, such openings, strategically placed, can give you the best of both worlds – a sense of connection at the same time as a separation of activities. Openings can be any shape or size: long thin vertical gaps running floor to ceiling, round portholes or horizontal windows.

Interior glazing – in the form of glass doors, screens and room dividers – also has a lightening effect. It is very important, however, when extending glass down to floor level, whether in the form of French windows, internal doors or transparent partitions, to make sure that you use toughened safety glass, which fractures into harmless smooth-edged pebbles when broken rather than into lethal shards.

Even more dramatic, although a little vertiginous, are glass floors. You can install a small section of glass flooring at an upper level to provide top lighting for the lower storey; glass walkways also minimize the impact of a mezzanine level inserted in a double-height space. Again, the type of glass is critical: the usual specification is a 2cm (¾in) top layer laminated to a 1cm (½in) base. Flooring glass is generally available in 1m-square (3ft 3in-square) panels and comes with sandblasted friction bars or dots to reduce slipperiness.

Glass block, the structural form of the material, is very useful for creating internal windows and partitions, particularly when it comes to screening areas where you require privacy, such as bathrooms and showers. It is not strictly necessary to provide a window in a bathroom, although there must be adequate ventilation. Where a bathroom does lack natural light, partition walls of obscured glass or glass block can be a good way of improving light conditions without baring all. Alternatively, you might opt for the very latest high-tech solution – a glass screen that incorporates photovoltaic cells and which can be transformed from transparent to opaque at the flick of a switch when you require privacy.

Open staircases, either cantilevered or suspended, provide minimal interruption of light and views. If you do not want a fully open staircase (if you have young children to consider, for example), you can replace the risers with glass or transparent Perspex for a similar effect.

Direction

Many people are entirely unaware of which direction different rooms in their home face and yet orientation has a profound effect on the quality of natural light. It is easy enough to appreciate that rooms on upper storeys are more likely to be lighter and brighter than those that are at ground or semi-basement level, but what difference does it make if a room in your house faces east or west, north or south? (For 'north' read 'south' and vice versa in the southern hemisphere.)

• North- and northeast-facing rooms receive little direct sunlight. Light remains fairly even in intensity throughout the day and there are no strong shadows. The light itself is cool and whitish in tone, which means colours are perceived more accurately. Artists have long valued north light because it allows them to continue working for longer under relatively stable light conditions. For living areas, however, north light can be harsh and inhospitable. It needs to be warmed up with colours from the warm end of the spectrum – creams, yellows, pinks and reds – and it needs warm artificial light sources – tungsten bulbs and lamps diffused in warm-toned shades – to create a more welcoming and livable atmosphere.

• East-facing rooms are the first to receive light in the morning. Light levels are warm and bright until midday, after which shadows increase. Direct light disappears later in the day.

• West-facing rooms do not receive direct sunlight until midday, after which light is warm and bright. In the late afternoon, shadows lengthen and light levels decrease.

• South- and southwest-facing rooms are warmly lit all day. As a consequence, such areas are also more likely to heat up quite dramatically, a factor that can be exploited in passive energy strategies. Glare may be a problem when the sun is at its strongest around midday. Because the light is naturally warm in tone, cool colours, such as blues, blue-greens and lilacs are particularly effective and will help to make a room feel more spacious.

Whenever possible, try to allocate uses to rooms according to their orientation. You would not expect a climbing plant that prefers a southerly aspect to do well planted against a north-facing wall. Similarly, situating a kitchen in a semi-basement that faces north will not give you optimum conditions in which to work. We tend not to spend much time in our bedrooms during the day, but are most sensitive to the quality of light we experience first thing in the morning. For this reason, choosing a bedroom that faces east can help to start you off on the right foot each day.

Creating new openings

Whenever people plan extensions or significant alterations to their home that involve structural work, more often than not they take the opportunity to create large openings that blur the boundary between inside and out. At least part of the instinct that lies behind that ever-popular home improvement, the addition of a conservatory, must be the desire to bring more natural light into the home. Part- or fully glazed extensions, garden rooms and French doors that connect kitchens to outside areas are direct ways of increasing natural light in areas of the home that are most frequently used.

Previously, rooms or additions that featured expanses of glass, particularly overhead in the form of glazed roofs, suffered extremes of temperature. While glare and overheating could be mitigated by blinds and ventilation during the summer, winter saw an inevitable rise

in fuel bills if such areas were to remain habitable. In recent years, however, a new type of glass has been developed that allows light through but prevents heat from escaping. Low-emissivity (low-E) glass has a thin coating of silver oxide that reflects infrared energy back into the interior. In warm climates, the glass can be fitted the other way round so the interior is kept cool. Low-E glass is more expensive than standard but saves money in reduced energy costs over time.

Another popular form of home improvement is the attic or loft conversion, which necessitates the installation of rooflights or skylights to make a habitable room. Even if you are not converting your attic, however, adding a rooflight can dramatically improve the quality of natural light, especially in hallways and stairs where there might not be much in the way of direct natural light. Daylight that comes from above is naturally uplifting and fosters an airy, expansive feeling.

There are several different types of roof window: the skylight that is generally unopenable and which is fitted into a flat or sloping plane of the roof; the rooflight, which is generally fitted into a sloping plane and is openable for

ventilation; and the sun scoop. The sun scoop is a way of bringing natural light through a void, such as a roof space, and delivering it where it is needed. It consists of a wide tube with a highly reflective interior, one end of which protrudes through the roof like a shallow domed porthole, with the other end flush with the ceiling where light is to be targeted.

Other relatively simple alterations include increasing the size of existing windows. The most straightforward way is to lengthen a window by taking out the portion of wall under the sill, which has no impact on the structure of your house.

Opposite: *Natural light that comes from above generates a great sense of wellbeing and also creates ideal working conditions for activities that require special concentration. At ground or lower levels, however, the condition and amount of natural light can be less than ideal. Here, adding a kitchen extension has provided the opportunity to introduce a skylight that bathes the kitchen preparation area below in full daylight.*

Above: *A large pane of glass has been installed in the sloping plane of the roof to bring light into a converted attic. Glazing on this scale is heavy, however, and you may need to consult an engineer to determine how to strengthen the existing roof structure in order to provide adequate support.*

Left: *The secret of lighting space successfully is to avoid glare. Glare arises when there are too few light sources and where each source is too bright, setting up tiring contrasts of light and dark. Here, soft and subtle light bounced off smooth white planes imparts a restful atmosphere.*
Opposite: *Central or overhead fixtures should be avoided in bedrooms, wherever possible, because they cause glare, particularly when viewed from a prone position. Here, strip lighting concealed behind the top of fitted storage washes the ceiling with light, while bathroom lighting is diffused through a glazed door.*

Lighting space

Artificial light is what we rely on when natural light levels are too low to perform everyday routines and tasks safely and effectively. More creatively, a lighting scheme should also be designed to enhance existing architectural details, to bring out the best features of the interior and to help to ameliorate any shortfalls in proportion, scale or size.

Well-designed lighting has the potential to provide atmosphere and depth even in the most unremarkable of surroundings; poor or insensitive lighting, on the other hand, can strip even the most beautifully proportioned and detailed space of every last vestige of character and comfort. The killer, in many cases, is the dreaded central fixture. Bright overhead light is banal, depressing and tiring, because it is both glaring and utterly uniform – we may have to tolerate it in supermarkets and even put up with it in our doctor's waiting rooms, but we certainly should not have to do so in our own home where we can exercise some choice.

space

Glowing backgrounds

In terms of how we experience space, lighting plays two important roles. First of all, it is descriptive, revealing form, volume and detail to a greater or lesser degree, and, secondly, it is atmospheric, determining how we interpret what we see as well as how we feel about it. In most areas of the home, there is a need for a certain amount of focused or directional light to support different activities or pick out points of visual interest. By and large, however, successful spatial lighting relies on ambient or background sources.

The best ambient lighting tends to be lighting that you don't see. What you see instead are soft, glowing planes – walls, ceilings and even floors that are gently illuminated and shadow-free. To achieve this quality, the light fixtures themselves need to be discreetly positioned – generally hidden or recessed – so that it is the reflected light and not the source itself that is visible. Bouncing light off reflective or semi-reflective planes in this way is the same type of strategy as employing 'fill' lighting in the theatre, or the use of silvered dishes to diffuse light in still photography: it helps to set the scene.

Because this type of approach can be achieved only with multiple light sources, you immediately avoid the deadening effect that comes when you rely solely on a single overhead light to provide background illumination. Multiple sources mean there are no dead zones where the light does not reach and no harsh shadows to generate unease. Each one of these sources can be fitted with bulbs of relatively low wattage and the combined effect will still be as bright as, if not brighter, than relying on a single, glaring overhead source. At the same time, because each light is not overly bright, you will avoid the risk of glare by reducing the contrast between each individual light and its surroundings. Put all the lighting sources for one room on dimmer controls and you have an instant way of varying light levels, and therefore mood, according to the time of day and the occasion.

Lighting that relies to such an extent on the quality of surfaces and planes is consequently highly affected both by types of finish and by decorative choices. The more reflective a finish, the brighter and sharper the light. Expanses of glass and metal as well as glossy or lacquered paint finishes spread the light around and promote a sparkling effect. Light reflected off matt surfaces, such as plaster and wood, is softer and more diffused. By the same token, any light that is reflected in this way is also fairly revealing of the quality of surfaces and finishes – if plasterwork is a bit battered and cracked, such imperfections will show up all too clearly.

Proportion, scale and volume

Our eyes are naturally attracted by light. Go into a room in the daytime when there are no lights switched on and your attention will be drawn first of all to the window as the principal light source. You can make use of this natural predisposition to follow the light by arranging your lighting scheme so that it accentuates the best features of the interior and literally directs the eye to what you want it to be looking at. When light is bland and even, as is the case where there is a dominant or sole central fixture, rooms lose any inherent interest: there is no emphasis and so everything looks the same.

Bouncing light off the planes of the walls and the ceiling is the most effective way of playing around with proportion and scale. Light a room exclusively from the centre and you cast shadows into the corners and make the room seem smaller, lower and more enclosed.

Opposite: The sculptural planes of a staircase are emphasized by concealed lighting that has been carefully positioned in order to bring out the curved forms. Additional illumination is provided by individual lights inset in the stair treads. This type of lighting scheme is much more effective where the surfaces and finishes to be highlighted are smooth and unbattered.

By contrast, directing ambient light at a ceiling plane literally lifts the lid off a room. Directing light at the floor makes furniture and built-in units appear to lift and float; while if you wash the walls with light, a room will feel much more spacious, as if the basic structure of the space has been pushed back as far as the boundaries will allow.

This type of strategy is also a good way of accentuating architectural detail or period features, such as cornicing and decorative mouldings. In plainer, more contemporary settings, planes of light bring crisp, sculptural architectural form into relief.

You can make use of the same basic principle when it comes to external lighting, particularly for paved or terraced areas that are directly connected to the house and are visible through large expanses of glass or glazed garden doors. Lighting a terrace or external walls in a gentle wash of light has the effect of borrowing space by visually extending the interior into outdoor areas. This effect is heightened if the internal flooring treatment and the exterior paving are similar in tone, so there is less sense of interruption.

While many of us tend to think about room sizes in terms of square metres (or square feet) – the basic dimensions of width and length – architects like to talk about spatial 'volume', which also takes height into account. When you diffuse light over walls and ceilings, you automatically heighten the appreciation of space as volume. The effect is even more pronounced where areas that are very different in volume adjoin each other. Part of the unconscious pleasure we gain from our experience of space is derived from contrast and variety, such as when we move from small, relatively enclosed areas into loftier, more expansive ones. Lighting that emphasizes volume brings a certain theatricality into play.

Choosing fittings

When it comes to creating atmospheric, glowing backgrounds, any fitting that can be directed so that light bounces off the walls, the ceiling or, indeed, the floor is ideal; also suitable are wall fittings that emit a diffused light that is largely omnidirectional. Many of these are discreet, if not minimal, in appearance. However, bear in mind that this type of lighting does demand careful planning. Recessed or concealed ambient lighting is difficult and disruptive to install once final wall, ceiling and floor finishes are in place.

Uplighting can be achieved in a variety of ways: by the use of floor-standing uplights or uplights recessed into the floor, by standard lamps whose shades direct light exclusively upwards and by wall-mounted uplights. One of the most common mistakes people make with uplighting, particularly in the case of wall-mounted uplighters, is to position them too close to the ceiling, where they have next to no effect. If the room in question has a low ceiling, opt for floor-standing or recessed uplights instead.

Spotlights, either single spotlights strategically placed, or track lighting, can be angled to wash walls and ceilings with light, or to fill in dark corners. You will need to experiment with positioning to achieve the optimum effect and to avoid creating hotspots of glare, especially if you are lighting highly reflective finishes. Ceiling-mounted or recessed spots obviously offer a limited degree of uplighting; the most you are going to get is a graze of light along the ceiling plane. Where there are lower beams or an exposed roof structure, however, spots can be fixed to these and directed so that their light shines upwards.

A variant on the spotlight is the wall-washer, which is specifically designed to bathe the wall in soft, even light. These are usually ceiling-mounted and they may either swivel so that

Opposite: Multiple sources of light, well-concealed, give the interior a great sense of vitality. Here, lighting concealed behind the ceiling planes creates a lit strip of diffused illumination overhead. A similar effect outlines the chimney breast, while downlights target the seating areas. More localized light is provided by a pair of table lamps placed either side of the fireplace.

the direction of light can be adjusted, or may include baffles or incorporate hinged side panels so that the spread of light can be carefully controlled and directed.

Wall lights include those that are directional to a greater or lesser degree, such as wall-mounted uplights, and those that are not. Into the latter category fall a wide range of designs, both period and contemporary, where the light source is diffused by some form of shade or covering, either so that it emits a soft glow or so that light spills out top and bottom and is reflected off the wall. Because wall lights tend to be used in multiples – most typically in pairs – you inevitably achieve a livelier form of background lighting than if you were relying on a central source.

POINTS TO CONSIDER

• Reduce or eliminate dependence on overhead or central ceiling fixtures as a source of background light. See also 'Creating a focus' (pages 76–83) for ways of using central lighting in rooms more successfully.

• Wash walls and ceilings with light if you want to increase the sense of height and spaciousness.

• Multiple, relatively low-level individual sources of light reduce the risk of generalized glare.

• Target light at architectural details worthy of attention, such as cornicing, mouldings and fireplaces.

• Pale-toned decoration, the more pristine the better, enhances the effect of good lighting.

Creating a focus

There are many situations and occasions when it is important to use lighting to create a focus – whether it is to draw people together in relaxed conversation groups or to encourage a welcoming, convivial mood around a dining table. Focus implies a centre of some sort, which might be seen to suggest a return to the central light, with all its considerable drawbacks. However, central lighting can be successful in certain situations if you are very careful about the way you use it and the type of fitting you choose.

Focal points tap into our basic human instinct to gather around sources of light and warmth – and nothing holds a greater attraction in this respect than a real fire. By contrast, rooms that are entirely evenly lit can have something of an institutional quality, which has the potential to leave people marooned in their own separate spaces.

Successful central lighting

Central lights, whether ceiling-mounted or pendant, linger on in many homes. In older properties, the central light is generally a throwback to a time when gas, rather than electricity, was the principal means of illumination; however, many new homes also feature central lights as a standard, even in living areas.

As mentioned in the previous section (see pages 72–4), a central fixture should never be employed as the sole source of light in any part of the home where the emphasis is chiefly on relaxation, and there is also a good argument for doing without it altogether in bedrooms, where it creates far too dominant and glaring an effect when you are lying in bed. Although central light is perfectly practical in utility areas, it provides less effective working conditions in kitchens, where light needs to be much more targeted and where there might otherwise be a risk that you could be working in your own shadow.

If you are going to have a central light, it should always be supplemented by other forms of background lighting, whether these are table or standing lamps, or uplighters, wall lights and spotlights. With much of the necessary ambient lighting coming from other sources, you can then afford to reduce the risk of uncomfortable glare by using a bulb of relatively low wattage in a central light without compromising light levels overall.

Because central lights are suspended overhead, there is a high risk of glare if the bulbs are not hidden from view or the light is not diffused in some way, and this is true even when you are using bulbs of relatively low wattage. Many central or pendant fixtures achieve the necessary diffusion by enclosing the light source completely in a shade – the ubiquitous Japanese paper lantern is a very good example. The larger the shade, the greater the degree of diffusion. Pendants with dished shades that reflect light upwards also reduce the risk of glare. Alternatively, if the design of the fitting means the bulb will be necessarily exposed, you can use a crown-silvered bulb to direct the light upwards.

In living areas – and often in hallways, too – the chief role of a central light nowadays is a decorative one. Fittings such as chandeliers, pierced lanterns inset with coloured glass and contemporary sculptural designs provide a focus of interest because of their form and colour, rather than the quality or direction of the light they emit. When you are choosing

Opposite: *Traditional chandeliers feature faceted glass or crystal drops and ropes of beads that catch the light. Such period-style fittings do not necessarily require a complementary context: the clash of old and new can be very effective.*

Left: *Ingo Maurer is one lighting designer who has never entirely abandoned the chandelier form. This witty design called 'Zettel'z' (1997) suspends 'love letters' written in different languages around a frosted halogen bulb and a parabolic reflector.*

Above: *Three simple round paper lanterns suspended at staggered heights ring the changes on the standard central fixture.*

a central light, look out for those that will continue to have as much impact, decoratively speaking, when they are not illuminated as they do when they are switched on.

It is also important to remember that you will be able to see a central light in a hallway or landing from different levels on a stairway – from above as you descend, then sideways on, and then from below when you reach the bottom of the staircase. Any fitting where the bulb is exposed at any of these vantage points will inevitably cause glare.

Chandeliers and other branched fittings make stunning decorative features. As they incorporate many points of light, rather than a single source, they are naturally less likely to cause glare than other types of central fitting. A fully lit chandelier, however, can be an overly dazzling object. One solution is to put it on a dimmer control. Downlights or spotlights that are trained on the chandelier itself will also enhance its decorative impact by accentuating the shape of the individual glass or crystal elements.

Individual focal points

Wherever people gather – to sit and talk or to enjoy a meal – is a natural focus that needs the supplement of light. The main role of lighting in these situations is to generate a sense of intimacy and to draw people together. In this sense, it is background light, but of a very local nature. Local light cannot be considered without close reference to furniture arrangement – if you provide local light where people are not able to sit, you are sending out a mixed message which may result in feelings of vague unease, as if different elements of the interior are somehow warring with each other.

Table and standing lamps, judiciously placed, are invaluable when it comes to creating individual focal points. The soft, diffused pool of light that they produce illuminates people's faces evenly and describes an inclusive circle. Similarly, by placing lights strategically so that the eye is led onwards in a natural progression, you can animate the interior with vitality. When you are planning a lighting scheme, it is easy to overlook the fact that for much of the time we do not experience space in a static way: we move from area to area within a room, from room to room, and up and down the stairs. Think about arranging the lighting so that it is not all at the same position on the vertical axis – not all at head height, or table height, for example – in order to create a more varied 'skyline' that you can appreciate from different postures. At the same time, avoid cluttering up an interior with too many freestanding lights, particularly if they are very different in style.

As freestanding lights, both table lamps and standing lamps need to be plugged into sockets that are relatively close at hand so that flexes do not trail across the floor where they might present a hazard and cause a fall. Many homes have power points only around the periphery of the room, which can limit the positioning of these fittings. Because we like to position light beside sofas and chairs, in turn this can result in a rather static wall-hugging room arrangement. One solution is to install a couple of floor sockets in the centre of the room so that seating groups can be pulled away from the walls. Floor and table lamps are eminently portable, which means if you decide to change your room around at some future time, you do not need to rethink your entire lighting scheme. This is all the more reason for making sure you have enough sockets where you need them at the outset of planning a room.

Right: *An overscaled floor-standing lamp provides light for a seating area. Adjustable lights are particularly useful in this situation, as you can vary the height or location of the light source to avoid glare. Similarly, portable lamps do not commit you to a fixed furniture arrangement.*

An undeniable focus of attention is the dining table. In purely practical terms, we need a certain level of light to be able to see what is on our plates. Whether we eat in a separate dining room, in the kitchen or in part of a living area or multipurpose space, that degree of light will normally be supplied by existing background lighting. What we also need, however, is emotional lighting, the sort that transforms what might otherwise be refuelling into a social occasion.

Lighting a dining area presents something of a challenge. To create a hospitable mood that draws people in, light must be directed at the table, which means an overhead fitting. The risk of this arrangement is, of course, glare. If the light is too

bright and too broad in its spread, it will work against any feeling of intimacy and harsh shadows will be cast on faces. Similarly, if the light source is visible, you will be conscious that there is something directly overhead that you are trying to avoid looking at. The ideal is to direct light chiefly at the centre of the table, so that it reflects upwards, lighting faces sympathetically. Dimmer controls always extend flexibility, but they are particularly invaluable in dining areas, enabling you to match the light level to the occasion and the time of day.

Pendants are a popular choice for lighting dining tables. Choose a design that has a deep shade that conceals the bulb so that the light source is not visible. Alternatively,

Opposite: *Lighting a dining table can be tricky because of the risk of glare. The solution is to direct light at the centre of the table so that it reflects back up into people's faces. Pendant fittings should be deep enough to conceal the light source. The deep shades shown here are ideal for the purpose and deliver a soft diffusion of light. More than one pendant is a good idea if the table is long and rectangular; circular tables, on the other hand, will probably need only one.*

Above left: *A deep conical shade is positioned over the centre of the dining table, while Castiglione's classic modern design 'Arco', which in fact was originally designed to light dining tables, is here used to illuminate a seating area. 'Arco', designed in 1962, features a curved steel stem counterweighted by a marble block.*

Above right: *One of Noguchi's 'Akari' lanterns gives a warm diffusion of light in a seating area. The mulberry paper shade ensures there is no risk of glare.*

spotlights and downlights that emit much narrower beams of light can be positioned so that the centre of the table, rather than the diners' heads, is illuminated. The ultimate emotional light is, of course, candlelight, which makes an unbeatable accompaniment to a celebratory meal.

POINTS TO CONSIDER

• In living areas, always fit central lights with bulbs of relatively low wattage and then supplement them with other forms and sources of background light.

• Choose central lights for their decorative interest, rather than for their impact on overall levels of illumination.

• Put chandeliers on dimmers or spotlight them to bring out and draw attention to their visual appeal.

• Provide local light for conversation areas and any places where people naturally gather.

• Consider installing floor-level power points in the centre of a room to permit more dynamic furniture arrangement.

• Reinforce a sense of progression by providing lights at strategic points and at different heights.

• Direct light at a dining table so that it shines in the centre and then reflects upwards.

• Make sure the light sources are concealed if you are using pendant fixtures over a dining table.

Light and shadow

On the face of it, shadow might be seen to represent a failure of lighting, and it is true that there are many contexts in which it is less than welcome and, indeed, hazardous. Obscuring shadows on the stairs that do not allow you to distinguish readily between tread and riser can lead to accidental tumbles. Shadowed kitchen work surfaces or hobs can be similarly dangerous when you are handling sharp knives or hot pans, while shadows that fall across the pages of a book or a computer screen will lead to eyestrain. However, aside from these specific shortfalls in basic practicality in the home, in most other contexts shadow remains an indispensable element in creating evocative lighting schemes.

If light is what reveals the world to us, shadow describes it in greater detail. It is through shadow that we appreciate the mass, heft and three-dimensional form of objects, and through it that we also come to sense the material quality and textures of different surfaces without even touching them. Shadow, as much as light, can be used as a powerful way of creating mood and atmosphere – even a little theatricality.

Atmosphere and spatial quality

Shadowed areas are inherently mysterious, even a little melancholy. In extreme circumstances, where shadows are very heavy or well defined, the mood tends towards the menace of the thriller or *film noir*, where the villain's face is banded by starkly contrasting stripes of light and dark, or the bright light that appears at the head of an exceptionally dark staircase suggests that something evil might be lying in wait.

Devotees of the Gothic aside, most people do not want to invest their home with such an atmosphere of high drama and suspense. Nevertheless, some degree of shadow is essential if there is to be any atmosphere at all. The answer is not to opt for great contrasts of light and dark, which are tiring on the eyes and which can generate unease, but to create a more balanced and gradual effect between softly lit areas and softly shadowed ones. You can play around with this balance more effectively if lights are individually dimmable, or if there are two or more dimmable lighting circuits within a given area.

The conventional way of using dimmers is to turn down the lights when it is still relatively bright outdoors and then gradually raise the levels as darkness falls. This may be sensible and beneficial in practical terms, for example in kitchens where lighting illuminates a working area. However, in living areas the reverse can be more atmospheric, particularly if there are expanses of window which are left unscreened after dark. Dimming the lights as it grows darker outside helps to keep the mood relaxed and intimate.

Shadow, as much as light, is a means of altering the way we appreciate spatial quality. To take the example of a wall that comprises a chimney breast flanked by two shallow alcoves or recesses, you can achieve very different effects depending on where the light and shadows fall. Light the chimney breast, leaving the alcoves in shade, and the entire wall will seem to advance; light the alcoves, on the other hand, and the wall will seem to recede and the room will appear more spacious. The same orchestration of light and dark can bring about the sculptural modelling of contemporary interiors that might otherwise be lost

shadow

if the light was uniformly even. At the same time, if light is a way of directing one's attention to and highlighting the best features of the interior, shadow is a useful means of drawing a merciful veil over anything that might be less than ideal in a particular space.

Where the shadow assumes even greater importance is in the garden. As the garden writer and presenter Monty Don has written in connection with this same issue, 'darkness is personal'. An overlit garden is not only contributing to general light pollution but can be an affront to the sensibilities of neighbours, who might prefer to experience their own gardens under more evocative conditions than the stark glare of light spill. In this context, bright light is nothing less than an invasion of space, because it destroys any sense of seclusion, which is an important part of what we value about our gardens. It might even be argued that shadow is what garden lighting is all about. Low lights, placed at intervals some distance apart from each other, accentuate and silhouette foliage and branches without obliterating the deep, mysterious areas of shade that lie between them. Similarly, lights positioned so that they pick out a path, rather than illuminating the whole of it at once, entice us onwards.

Texture and form

Less overt than colour and pattern, texture is nevertheless a key element in interior design, arising naturally through the interplay of different surfaces, finishes and materials. A room that is entirely decorated in smooth matt surfaces runs the risk of appearing a little soporific and banal, just as one that exclusively features expanses of highly reflective glass and metal can seem a little too hectic and energized. Textural variety, on the other hand, gives character and depth, along with a human dimension in its invitation to touch.

Where surfaces and finishes are overtly textured, skimming them with light brings out this extra dimension, with shadows defining each dent, dip or hollow. An exposed brickwork wall, tongue-and-groove panelling, mosaic and tilework immediately become much livelier surfaces when light is slanted across them to reveal their inherent rhythm.

Shadow also has an important role to play when it comes to revealing form. Evenly illuminated on all sides, objects lack a certain presence. When lit more directionally, their shape and form is thrown into relief by the modelling of shadows, a particularly evocative effect in decorative displays.

Left: Natural forms, such as trees and plants, always create interesting shadows. You can exploit this effect by uplighting or sidelighting indoor plants; similarly, in the garden, lighting shrubbery and other types of low-level planting from below or to the side is much more evocative than directing light from above, which tends to flatten shape and reduce detail.

Above: Textured surfaces, such as this painted brick wall, have a tactile quality that can be emphasized by lighting. One of the easiest ways to do this is to direct light across the surface so that shadows dip and fall into gaps and spaces.

Right: *While contemporary tastes tend towards light, bright interiors, those that are more dimly lit and shadowy have a greater sense of intimacy. Here, there is the best of both worlds: a snug bedroom with dark-toned walls and wood-clad ceiling is fully open to the outdoors.*

Filtering the light

Light sources, both the natural and the artificial sort, can be filtered to conjure a kind of shadowplay, which brings a kinetic dimension to the interior. In the case of windows and glazed openings, slatted blinds, louvred shutters, etched glass and lace all serve to make intriguing patterns of light and shade, which are further animated by changing light conditions throughout the day.

Many light fittings – particularly more decorative varieties – are effectively more about shadow than they are about light. Tord Boontje's 'Garland', which encircles a bulb with a filigree of delicate metal foliage, is an obvious example (see page 85). In the case of children's carousel lights, the shadows cast on the wall are every bit as appealing as the bright, moving scenes. Philippe Starck's black chandelier for the Baccarat headquarters in Paris is a stunning example of an attraction of opposites. Less dramatically, many light fittings, from pendants to table lamps, incorporate shades that filter light through pinholes, starry cutouts or mesh.

POINTS TO CONSIDER

• Avoid obscuring shadows in working areas, on stairs and any other location where they might constitute a hazard. This is particularly important in households where there are children or elderly people. Bear in mind that as we age we require much higher levels of light to navigate obstacles safely and perform tasks effectively.
• Exploit the graduating contrast between light and shade to enhance spatial quality.
• In areas devoted to relaxation, use dimmers to adjust the balance between natural and artificial light.
• Keep the light levels low in garden lighting. Intriguing shadows are more sympathetic. Overlighting is a nuisance for neighbours and contributes to light pollution.
• Gently graze light over attractively textured surfaces for added depth of character.
• Directional light helps to bring out the shape and form of decorative objects.
• Create patterns of light and shade by filtering both natural and artificial light sources.

Inset opposite: *'IPCO Sphere' (2001) designed by Ron Arad is a fibreglass and polyester sphere pierced with pinholes and fitted with an ordinary incandescent bulb. Based on the principle of the camera obscura, it projects images of the bulb's filament onto walls and ceiling.*

Left: *Windows screened by slatted or louvred blinds dapple a room with patterns of light and shade. Where windows face in different directions, the effect of the shifting patterns is particularly evocative as the sun moves across the sky during the course of the day.*

Above: *Moorish-style star lanterns transform a hallway into a magical light show. Such an effect might be too insistent and ultimately tiring in a living area, but in linking areas such as halls, stairs or landings that are passed through momentarily, they can be very charming.*

Defining with light

Within most areas of the home' there will be one or two particular elements that require – or deserve – the additional definition provided by a targeted boost of light. In working areas, it will be desktops, worktops and counters; in living areas, there may be decorative displays or features that are worth emphasizing. Lighting can also be used to pick out routes through a space, or to accentuate large fitted units and fixtures or freestanding pieces of furniture.

On its own, this type of lighting is not enough to support general activities within any particular room. Because the light is generally highly directional, there will be too great a contrast between the lit area and its surroundings unless ambient or background lighting is also in place. On the other hand, even a room that has a good quality of background lighting can benefit greatly from the extra definition that this type of lighting provides. Accent, task or architectural light all serve to sharpen and focus attention, giving a sense of depth and contrasting layers to a lighting scheme.

Task lighting

While accent light may be optional, task lighting is not. The task in question may be the very serious business of earning your living from home, or it may simply be reading a book or magazine for relaxation; it may be cooking and food preparation, or shaving or putting on make-up. These many diverse activities in the home that demand close attention require targeted, supplementary light.

Whatever the task, the essential element is to make sure the working area is shadow-free as well as brightly lit. If you light a desk with an overhead light or series of downlighters, for example, there is always the chance that your own head, arm or upper body might cast shadows on the page or keyboard. Similarly, many people install track or spotlighting in the kitchens, but at too great a distance from the counter or hob for the working area to be illuminated directly. Where the light source is coming from above and behind, you will inevitably be working in shadow.

In the case of desk work, you need a task light positioned to one side, angled so that light falls unimpeded on the focus of attention. Flexible, movable lights are ideal, particularly for

Right: *For an extra boost of illumination beside the bed, you can choose from any number of types of lamps and fittings: simple shaded bedside lamps, angled desk lights, wall-mounted adjustable fittings or, as here, a softly diffused pendant suspended low beside the bed.*

computer work; those where the bulb is deeply recessed within the shade prevent any risk of glare. The same principle applies when you are reading, whether you are sitting in a chair or propped up in bed. Light should come from the side, over the shoulder, so that it falls on the pages of the book. In the case of bedside lights, those that incorporate flexible or repositionable arms are very useful, as this enables you to move the light when you shift your reading position to maintain a comfortable pose, as you inevitably will.

Lighting working areas in kitchens demands very careful positioning. Unless your kitchen is very narrow, a centrally positioned track will cause overshadowing. The answer is to install fitted or recessed ceiling lights closer to the counter so that light can bounce off the wall or reflect from wall-hung units. You may need track or recessed spots in other parts of the kitchen as well, to illuminate ovens, fridges, central islands or built-in units. Installing a series of individual downlights or strip lights under wall cupboards provides an added degree of illumination for work surfaces, while many ventilation and extraction hoods also incorporate downlights arranged to shine directly over the hob.

In bathrooms, it is the mirror that requires the brightest illumination to support the activities of shaving and putting on make-up. Here, too, it is shadow that you should endeavour to avoid, particularly the hard shadows cast on the face from an overhead light – we may sometimes feel a bit grim in the morning, but there's no reason why we should look worse than we actually do. The minimum you will need is a pair of lights, either to each side or above and below the mirror. Some contemporary bathroom mirrors incorporate an extremely useful continuous light all the way around the perimeter or circumference.

Many utility areas, such as laundry rooms, do not require specific task lighting; others do. If you have a home workshop where you are going to be operating machinery or engaged in work that requires fine concentration, such as sewing, you will need task light just as much as in other working areas in the home. Clip-on spots, strip lights mounted in shelves or concealed behind baffles, as well as standard portable task lights such as the classic anglepoise, are all good inexpensive solutions for these workaday areas.

Lighting displays, pictures and details

Fine decorative objects, paintings, prints and other works of art more than merit the extra attention that accent lighting provides, but you do not need to have amassed a collection of museum-quality pieces in order to explore its potential. Accent lighting can be as impromptu as a clip-on spot that directs attention to a cheery array of plates or jugs on a kitchen shelf, or it may be as considered as recessed downlights concealed in a fine purpose-built display cabinet. However it is achieved, the point is to pick out the object, painting or collection so that it stands out from its surroundings but does not shriek for attention in a blaze of illumination. In comparison with the more forthright requirements of task lighting, accent lighting should always be fairly low-level and its effects subtle but effective.

Fixed accent lighting, such as that supplied by downlights, uplights or concealed strip lights, commits you to reserving certain areas for decorative display, which may limit your opportunities for moving things around at a later date. Once you have installed a downlight in an alcove to spotlight a bowl, there is little point in subsequently deciding it might look better over by the window. Most of us, however, do have favoured areas for display – often along mantelpieces, on alcove shelving that flanks chimney breasts and in other prominent

Opposite: *Natural light provides ideal conditions for reading or concentrated work. Otherwise, a reading light should ideally be adjustable so that you can position it depending on your seating posture. Light should fall over one shoulder directly on the page; light that falls from behind will only make obscuring shadows on your reading matter.*

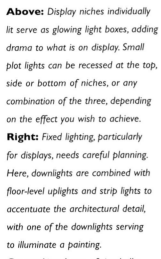

Above: Display niches individually lit serve as glowing light boxes, adding drama to what is on display. Small plot lights can be recessed at the top, side or bottom of niches, or any combination of the three, depending on the effect you wish to achieve.

Right: Fixed lighting, particularly for displays, needs careful planning. Here, downlights are combined with floor-level uplights and strip lights to accentuate the architectural detail, with one of the downlights serving to illuminate a painting.

Opposite: A row of tiny bulbs inset in a channel on the underside of a shelf adds dazzle and sparkle to a display of glass bowls.

positions where our treasured possessions can be appreciated. If you already have downlights installed in a room, you can take advantage of their inherently accenting quality by displaying objects in a location that is already targeted by the light they cast.

Before you decide on a fixed arrangement of accent lighting, play around with different lighting directions to see which most enhances the object in question. Downlighting is often very effective for delicate and transparent items; uplighting throws sculptural and textural qualities into high relief and makes objects look more imposing. Backlighting flattens shapes and creates interesting silhouettes, while sidelighting is more descriptive of contour and form. You can, of course, opt for a combination of lighting directions, a technique that is particularly effective where objects are displayed on glass shelves. It is also very unforgiving of dust and smears, however, so it is not for the faint-hearted.

Picture lighting can be achieved in a variety of ways, from the traditional small strip light attached to the frame or mounted on the wall just above it, to the angled 'eyeball' downlight or wall-washer recessed in the ceiling. There are several points to consider when lighting art. First of all, it is important to light the entire width and depth of the picture, not a portion of it; secondly, you need to arrange the lighting so that you avoid generating obscuring reflections on the picture glass, if any; and thirdly, you need to consider accurate colour rendition, which tends to mean choosing halogen over tungsten sources in the main.

Architectural lighting

What one might term 'architectural' lighting has increasingly come to play a more prominent role in contemporary domestic lighting schemes. Architectural lighting will often define certain features of the interior but is not necessarily directional; at the same time, it creates an ambient glow without spilling light very far. With this type of effect, lighting enters a more playful and unexpected realm.

Good examples of architectural lighting are individual lights recessed into the floor, stair treads or the base of the wall to pick out routes and pathways. Like downlights, which were once exclusively seen in retail outlets, floor lights are migrants from public spaces such as cinemas and theatres. Unlike downlights, however, which have become a little too ubiquitous in the home and are often used inappropriately, floor lights retain a freshness of appeal. In practical terms, they have obvious benefits, enabling dark halls or stairs to be safely and efficiently lit without the need to rely on wall fixtures or overhead lighting. At the same time, they are highly dramatic and exploit our natural tendency to let light lead us onwards. Recessed into the base of the wall, they create a gentle wash of light that picks out a hallway or stair treads; recessed in the floor, they emit a gentle uplight. This type of 'guiding' light has obvious applications in the garden, where it can be used to underscore the sense of progression between one discreet area and another.

Another form of architectural lighting relies on the use of concealed fittings, usually strip lights, to emphasize detail, built-in fixtures or large pieces of furniture. The basic principle is no more complicated than the standard strip light hidden behind a baffle at the base of kitchen wall units, but in recent years the application has broadened. At the base of beds, built-in storage units, plinths or room dividers, concealed strip lights serve to reduce the monumentality of such features and make them appear to float over the floor. Hidden behind cornices, the effect is similarly to create a visual distinction between the basic shell of the room and its fitted elements, while delivering a gentle wash of uplight that lifts the ceiling. Lights concealed within recesses or alcoves add a sense of crisp definition to architectural form. Backlit panels reduce the bulk of staple bathroom fixtures such as sinks and tubs, a particularly welcome effect where space is limited. All these effects can be considerably enhanced by colour, either by using a coloured light source itself, such as neon, or by means of a coloured filter over the bulb.

Above: *The crisp modelling of kitchen surfaces is picked out by concealed strip lighting.*
Below: *A rather unearthly effect is created by the use of strip lights hidden under the bed and built-in storage units in this bedroom, making them almost appear to hover over the fluffy shagpile carpet.*

Opposite: *Concealed lighting is a good way of describing and revealing architectural form. Here, lights hidden at the top and bottom of a shallow recess throw the sharp, clean lines of a custom-made bathroom sink into sharp relief, while providing a soothing, contemplative background.*

Above: *Cornices, alcoves, plinths, recesses and columns – indeed, any form of architectural modelling that interrupts the smooth plane of walls, ceiling or floor – provide perfect locations for concealing strip lights and an opportunity to introduce a gentle wash of defining light.*

right: *A glowing frame of concealed architectural light defines the ultra-sleek minimalist built-in storage that runs down the length of one wall of an all-white corridor. Far less minimal in style but equally successful in its effect is the decorative focal point of the exuberant contemporary chandelier suspended over the table in the adjoining dining room.*

Choosing fittings

Within this category of lighting, the emphasis is more on function than the appearance of the light itself. Although many desk lights, for example, are attractive in their own right – indeed, some are design icons – choosing the right fitting means considering the particular effect you are trying to create and making sure the fitting does its job.

Spotlights, downlights, uplights and strip lights are the workhorses of definition lighting. With directional light, one important aspect to consider is beam width. Beam width is determined by the fitting, the bulb and by attachments such as baffles and shutters. A narrow beam – typically 14 degrees – is ideal for picking out an object in a tight focus of attention. Wide beams (40 degrees) provide a greater spread of light, which may be required when lighting a picture.

Another element to consider is the colour of the light source. In many respects, halogen, particularly low-voltage halogen, scores over tungsten when it comes to definition lighting. The light is whiter and brighter, which is a positive asset for creating efficient working conditions; at the same time, halogen renders colours more faithfully, an advantage

when you are accenting decorative objects or paintings. The crispness of halogen complements contemporary styles of decoration and the materials – stainless steel, tile, glass and porcelain – commonly found in kitchens and bathrooms.

Strip lights have long been a popular choice for utilitarian lighting, in garages, workshops and similar behind-the-scenes locations. Many strip lights, however, are designed to be used in conjunction with fluorescent tubes, which can be problematic when you want to create a more evocative effect – fluorescent, despite continual improvements, retains a chilly, greenish colour cast and is not readily dimmable. Tungsten strips – also known as 'architectural tubes' – are not as long-lasting but produce a more sympathetic light.

POINTS TO CONSIDER

- Always combine directional or definition light with background lighting to avoid glare.
- Light working areas, counters and bathroom mirrors so that they are shadow-free.
- Flexible fittings are ideal for desk work and at chairside or bedside, as they allow ready repositioning.
- Think of the direction of light when accenting displays.
- Pick out architectural features, fixtures and fittings with recessed or concealed lights.
- Lights set at floor-level accentuate progression.
- Make sure light fittings provide the right degree of light spread for the area or object you are defining.
- Choose halogen over tungsten for working areas and displays; tungsten over fluorescent for strip lighting.

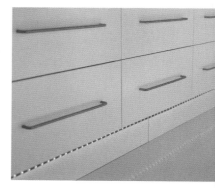

Above left: *Architectural or defining light need not necessarily be achieved through the use of strip lights. These individual lights that have been recessed into the floor at regular intervals mark out a pathway and are positioned close enough to the wall to throw the light upwards.*

Above: *A glowing strip of blue outlines a built-in storage unit. The lights are reflected in a narrow band of mirror inset into the floor.*

Opposite: *A similar effect is achieved used a rope light, where individual bulbs are encased in a plastic sheath.*

Decorative light may contribute to the overall lighting levels; often, however, it plays little or no practical role. Unlike ambient or task light, its purpose is not necessarily to provide enough illumination to work or even to see by. What it offers is a witty, intriguing and often theatrical celebration of light itself. A backlit panel enclosing a bathtub or fairy lights strung along a mantelpiece are ways of adding a special dimension to your interior.

In recent years, a new generation of lighting designers has brought a more creative approach into play, introducing a magical element to interior lighting schemes. Pieces such as Sharon Marston's fibre optic chandelier or Ingo Maurer's LED-studded glass table extend product design into a more lyrical realm.

with light

Points of light

Massed small points of light are immediately appealing. Unlike ambient lighting, which creates uniformly glowing planes, or directional light, where the beam is narrow and focused, points of light are both individual and collective in effect – the result is a field of light that is at the same time composed of distinct and discernible elements. In many such designs, each individual lamp emits only a small degree of light, which means there is no risk of glare, and hence no need to shade or diffuse the bulbs in any way.

What is so inherently beguiling about this form of lighting is the way in which it evokes a sense of wonder – the same response, perhaps, that one might have looking up at a star-filled night sky, or the child's open-mouthed delight at the first sight of a twinkling Christmas tree. There are other associations, as well, most particularly and perhaps most evocatively, with candlelight, a light source that is also dim enough not to require any degree of shading.

The archetypal form of massed points of light is the chandelier, which may have originally developed as a practical way of clustering candles to provide a burst of illumination in one place, but which quickly evolved into a decorative showpiece. With the development of new technologies and materials, contemporary designers have found seemingly endless ways of subverting this classic form, using strands of fibre optics, for example, or cascades of shimmering discs or beads. A famous example is by the noted German lighting designer Ingo Maurer. His 'LED Table' (2003) sandwiches tiny white LEDs (light-emitting diodes) between sheets of glass, arrayed in a pattern suggestive of the outline of a chandelier.

Points of light continue to have an undeniably celebratory association. In recent years, strings of fairy lights have increasingly refused to go back in the box with the rest of the Christmas decorations when the holiday season is over, but have remained on display all year round, trailed along mantelpieces, heaped in glass containers, or draped elegantly over mirror frames. Each tiny individual lamp emits very little heat, which means such strings of lights can be used in situations where other, hotter, lights would pose a serious fire hazard. Similarly, LEDs have thrown off their strictly functional role in computers and other similar electronic products to find exciting new applications in the creation of a diverse range of indoor starry effects.

Below: *In the past, chandeliers tended to be displayed in grand rooms and entrance halls. Today, they are equally often used to make an effective contrast of style or mood in simple or functional surroundings.*

Opposite: *After a few decades of eclipse, the chandelier is back in favour. Many contemporary designs are every bit as elaborate and eye-catching as traditional or period pieces. This confection, made of metal wire and delicate shards of recycled glass, pulls out all the stops.*

Chandeliers and branched fittings

Central or overhead fixtures might well have eventually disappeared from our homes almost completely were it not for the eternal popularity of the chandelier. Strictly defined, a chandelier is any fitting suspended from the ceiling that incorporates at least two or more candles or electric lamps. However, recent designs using fibre optics, LEDs and other technological innovations have broadened the concept considerably. In essence, a chandelier is a pendant fixture that generates the effect of many points of light.

In design circles, the chandelier fell out of favour about 20 years ago, its inherent busyness thought to be at odds with the clean, minimalist lines of contemporary décor. Recently, however, chandeliers, both traditional and modern in style, have gained a new lease of life and can now form the decorative focus of many otherwise understated spaces.

The basic form of the chandelier dates back centuries. The term itself comes from the French word for tallow candle (which was a low-quality candle made of animal fat); the earliest medieval examples consisted of candles stuck onto metal spikes, which in turn were mounted on cruciform wooden frames. As the centuries progressed, designs became ever more elaborate and theatrical, with the finest chandeliers being made of silver, glass and crystal. The renowned Venetian glassworks, Murano, has been particularly associated with glass chandeliers since 1700. From the eighteenth to the nineteenth century, chandeliers often featured cut lead crystal, the faceted drops and ropes of beads fracturing the light to form glittering centrepieces in grand hallways and reception rooms. Many of these were exceptionally heavy and required the ceiling joists to be reinforced with wooden blocks to support the weight. Lead in glass allows it to be cut more finely and results in a shimmering rainbow effect. The glamour and presence of these period fixtures have been wittily explored in Philippe Starck's recent design for Baccarat's flagship store in Paris, which features a chandelier lit by fibre optics suspended in a tank of water, a huge rotating chandelier weighing 700kg (1,545 tons) in the main stairwell, and a 'black' chandelier in the private dining room (black being an impossible colour to achieve in glass, the drops are actually a very dark red).

Original period examples can be found today in antiques shops or bought at auction; there are also a number of companies which still produce bespoke designs in the traditional way. Price varies, depending on the size and elaboration of the design, with the cheapest costing little more than any other 'designer' light fitting and the most expensive costing as much as a new car – a major outlay. Many of these can be customized. You might begin, for example, with a basic model and then gradually build up the ensemble with extra drops, crystals, ropes, glass flowers or fruits, as budget allows. Glass flowers and fruits are typically coloured which adds to the prettiness and charm; combined with twining gilt or painted metal branches, such confections have something of the enchanted forest about them.

Cheaper sources of the traditional-style chandelier include flea markets, secondhand shops for old versions and the high street for new productions. Factory-made repro chandeliers are widely available in the mass market.

In the past, large glass chandeliers were lit on rare occasions and shrouded in protective cloth bags when not in use. Staff cleaned them in situ. Today, chandelier specialists recommend dismantling the entire ensemble. First, take a photograph of the chandelier and label each strand; then dismantle it placing individual strands or drops in labelled

Opposite: *A string of fairy lights wrapped around a filigree metal armature makes an impromptu chandelier with many points of light. Feathers add a whimsical touch.*

Above: *A traditional candlelit chandelier, with drops and ropes of beads, echoes the architectural detailing of the cornicing and architraves. In contrast is the stark modernity of the stainless-steel kitchen workbench, a contemporary intrusion into the space.*

boxes to facilitate reassembly. It is not advisable to use spray cleaners; instead, wash the crystals in warm soapy water, rinse and dry with a soft, lint-free cloth.

As far as contemporary designs go, aside from a few notable examples, such as the Sarfatti pendant, a 30-bulb fitting designed in 1958 by Gino Sarfatti, modern designers resolutely eschewed the chandelier until relatively recently. Now, the branched, glittery form has been given a new and very desirable twist by contemporary designers.

In 2002, under the aegis of the creative consultant Ilse Crawford, the venerable Austrian crystal company Swarovski commissioned a number of contemporary designers to 'reinvent' the chandelier. The result was the 'Crystal Palace' collection, which featured work by Tord Boontje, Tom Dixon, Georg Baldele and Hella Jongerius, among others. Boontje's shimmering design was called 'Blossom', an asymmetric floral branch that is covered with twinkling LEDs.

Boontje's 'Wednesday Light', and its mass-market version 'Garland' that he produced for Habitat, is what one might call a 'deconstructed' chandelier. The effect of multiple points of light is generated very simply by a strand of leaf shapes in reflective metal that is draped around an ordinary bulb. The original version is constructed from stainless steel photographically etched at a precision medical instruments factory. The mass-market alternative is made of brass.

Other designs play around with the archetype in an amusing, often provocative way. 'ASA 100', for example, is a modern take on the chandelier, where the points of light are 100 small bulbs concealed within translucent empty plastic film canisters. '85 Bulbs' by Rodi Graumans is a cluster of bulbs suspended from a rose of plastic clip connectors, while the 'Wineglass' chandelier, designed by Gitta Gschwendtner and Carl Clerkin, features 18 wine glasses hung upside down surrounding a light source. Blurring the boundary between chandelier and single pendant light are designs such as 'Mr Bigoli', which consists of a mass of coiled spring tubing.

The lyrical work of British designer Sharon Marston turns the chandelier into a modern artform. With a background in jewellery and costume design, Marston uses woven nylon, polymer fibre optics, monofilament and polypropylene to produce one-off pieces that often feature organic petal or shell forms. Weaving with fibre optics allows her to create shimmering points of light that twinkle and change colour – more of a light experience than a light product.

Equally dramatic is Ron Arad's interactive 'Lolita' chandelier for Swarovski. Consisting of a spiral pixel board

mixing crystal with LEDs, its form resembles the descending tiers of the classic chandelier. A chandelier with a very modern difference, however: the spiral pixel board is capable of displaying text messages sent via SMS.

Scarcely chandeliers, but producing similar effects on a smaller scale, Swarovski also produces individual crystal plaques that fit over standard downlights. The result is to transform the rather monotonous appearance of downlighting into fractured points of light to wonderful effect.

Whether traditional or contemporary in style and effect, the chandelier is undoubtedly a showpiece. In the past, chandeliers were generally found in grand reception rooms, most particularly in lofty entrance halls, where they created an immediate impression on visitors and could be displayed to best advantage. Nowadays, people hang chandeliers wherever takes their fancy – in bedrooms for additional glitz; in bathrooms for a touch of tongue-in-cheek glamour; in dining areas to introduce a mood of celebration.

When you are deciding where to hang a chandelier to make the most of it, one of the most important aspects to consider is scale. The larger and more elaborate the design, the more space – that is, volume – it will require in order for its decorative effect to be properly appreciated. High-ceilinged rooms are ideal, or double-height spaces, such as open stairwells. There should be enough height for the chandelier to be hung at a sufficient drop so that it reads as an object in space; it is just as inappropriate to hang such a large piece too close to the ceiling as it would be to hang it too low overhead where it will interrupt views.

One obvious advantage of the chandelier is that it has decorative impact whether it is lit or not, which is why it is so useful for creating a focus of attention. You can enhance the effect by lighting the chandelier itself with directional spots or downlights, so that the crystal or glass glows and sparkles even when not switched on. It is also a good idea to reduce the risk of glare by putting the chandelier on a dimmer switch so that it is not overly dazzling when lit.

Opposite: *Moulded ceiling roses and medallions, particularly when surrounded by decorative cornicing, often look redundant without a central light. In this case, the fitting is a modern design, as much a sculptural mobile as a chandelier.*

Above left: *Traditional chandeliers feature faceted glass or crystal drops and ropes of beads that catch the light. Crystal, which can be more finely cut and which fractures the light into a multitude of glittery prisms, provides a more theatrical effect, but it is more expensive. However, you can always spread the cost of such a feature over time, starting with a basic ensemble and adding individual drops and ropes at a later date.*

Below left: *Manufactured by Flos, 'Taraxacum', a chandelier cum pendant light by celebrated lighting designer Achille Castiglioni, subverts the form by using many clear glass light bulbs instead of crystal drops. The basic structure is composed of 20 pressed and polished aluminium triangles that form the housing for 60 40-watt bulbs.*

Opposite: *A decorative period-style chandelier enclosed in a clear drum provides a very effective marriage of old and new, the simple lines of the shade containing and somewhat effacing the decorative exuberance of the fitting itself.*

Left: *Strings of fairy lights lend themselves to a variety of decorative effects. In combination with a divan draped with filmy muslin, the mood is definitely exotic, straight from A Thousand and One Nights.*

Opposite: *Because fairy lights emit so little heat they can be used safely and unshaded in almost any location. Here, twined around the banisters and branching over the wall on this landing, the sparkling points of light are evocative of an enchanted forest.*

Light strings and nets

Affordable, flexible and portable, light strings and light nets allow you to enjoy the charming effect of multiple points of light without the commitment, either of expense or placement, that the chandelier requires. Many of the designs are variations on the humble string of fairy lights.

Not so long ago, fairy lights had a limited seasonal outing, brought out with the tinsel and baubles to decorate the tree in December and packed away again by Twelfth Night. At some point, however, they stopped going back in the box and now they are the most popular ad hoc way of decorating with light. Cheap enough to add much-needed flair to the student bedsit, and versatile enough to complement any style of décor, from minimalist to maximalist, they can be used in a host of ways to lend a celebratory touch to the interior.

Light strings and light nets have a certain feel-good factor that makes them irresistible – in fact, in some homes, they tend to multiply. Memories of Christmas and other festivals are inevitably bound up with their appeal – at the darkest time of the year, bringing new light into the home instantly fills people with good cheer. At the same time, they are also suggestive of a different holiday mood, of warm relaxing evenings sitting in outdoor cafés and tavernas strung with lights.

There are a huge number of designs and styles on the market. Fairy lights can never really be considered minimalist in themselves, but plain strings of unshaded clear bulbs are about as simple as it gets. Strings of lights come in different lengths; some sets allow you to vary the effect, offering such features as random twinkling or strobing. Cabling tends to be either clear plastic or dark green, with the latter blending more unobtrusively with foliage and branches if you are using the lights to decorate a tree. The colour of the lamps is another variable; aside from the typical Christmas colour assortments of red and green, there are now many candy and fluorescent shades, including yellow, pink and turquoise.

Because each individual lamp gives out so little heat, fairy lights can be individually shaded with materials such as paper or fabric that would normally pose a fire hazard used in such close proximity to a light source. Fairy lights shaded with handmade paper flowers, lanterns or globes have an Eastern flavour. Otherwise, the choice is almost endless, everything from delicate dragonflies and leaf shapes to kitsch candy-coloured alphabets and glowing UFOs. Naturally enough, quite a significant number of designs available in the mass market display a Christmas theme – those strings of stars,

snowflakes and Santas that proliferate during the festive season may be welcome then, but you are unlikely to want to keep them up once the holiday is over.

Light nets and ropes can have year-round appeal. 'Neat', a popular Habitat design, consists of a mesh or net of small clear bulbs that can be hung on a wall or against a window, or even draped over shrubbery outdoors to brighten up your garden at night. The bulbs are replaceable, although they are very long-lasting in any case. Other variations on the theme include light 'ropes' where the bulbs or LEDs are fully encased in plastic tubing, and asymmetric branched strings of tiny bulbs that have a garland effect when draped.

When buying light strings or nets, make sure that the set conforms to safety standards. Read the safety instructions and keep them to hand. Many light strings and nets come with replacement bulbs, including a replacement fuse bulb; always replace any bulbs that have blown immediately to avoid overloading the set. Never cut the string or try to connect two strings together. Where strings or nets come

with a transformer, site it indoors and in a well-ventilated location – transformers get warm. Make sure cabling is kept well away from traffic routes to avoid tripping people up.

The teenage girl who still lurks in the heart of many of us may enjoy the 'fairy grotto' look, where less is never more, but light strings can also be used in more understated ways. Strings of lights lend themselves to linear effects, stretched along the length of a mantelpiece or shelf or trailed around an archway or mirror, while shaded light strings often look good hung vertically down the wall. A sinuous light rope, for example, might add just enough illumination to accent a decorative display on an otherwise underlit shelf. Because the lights require nothing more than a nearby socket, you can experiment with all kinds of different locations.

Fairy lights can also be bunched into glowing focal points, piled into glass containers or hearths. To make an ad hoc chandelier of your own, any light string gathered at a central point will do the trick, an effect equally successful whether you are using fairy lights or a string of small shaded lamps.

Opposite: *In the summer months, empty hearths can look a little forlorn. Fairy lights, which contribute light but not heat, are ideal for such locations. Here, wrapped around a decorative metal armature, they provide a glowing focal point.*

Left: *Light strings can be used in a linear fashion to outline shapes and define spaces. Wrapped around the supports of a child's platform bed, they softly illuminate the play space beneath. Children instinctively love sparkling lights; for some, it is an affection that is never quite outgrown.*

Below left: *There is something inherently tongue-in-cheek about light strings, a point wittily made here by trailing fairy lights around logs stacked in a hearth.*

Overleaf, left and right: *Fibre optics are increasingly being used by contemporary architects and designers to create dazzling effects. Here, individual strands of fibre optics dangle through a rectangle cut in the ceiling to make a breathtaking display of light and colour overhead.*

Another particularly evocative design is the 'e-candle' by designers Cholet and Le Deun of Arluminis. A candle with no fire, a light with no wire or switch, the candle's 'flame' is an LED that lights up at a touch. The light is powered by a mobile (cell) phone battery that lasts 80 hours.

LEDs can also be seen in the home in twinkling wall-mounted panels, part background light, part art installation. Some of these designs have different settings so that you can vary the effect, as well as separate speed controls.

Fibre optics

Once prohibitively expensive, which largely restricted its use to the commercial realm, fibre optics is another unusual light source that is increasingly finding its way into the domestic interior. Ideal for use in combination with water (see pages 146–9), it also allows the simulation of 'points of light' effects.

In fibre optics, the light source is a light box, located away from where the light is actually emitted. Light from the light box is directed at the bunched ends of coated strands of acrylic or fibreglass, then travels the length of these strands to emerge as small twinkling points of light. Because the light source is remote, there is no heat at the point where the light is emitted, and no risk of water coming in potentially lethal contact with electricity. For this reason, fibre optics is often used in museums or areas where delicate items, sensitive to heat or UV radiation, are on display, as well as in swimming pools and other watery locations. Fibre optics can also be effectively substituted for downlights in situations where it is undesirable to disrupt existing roof insulation.

For the majority of people, fibre optics is principally familiar in the form of the popular kitsch novelty lamps of the 1960s and 1970s, whose bristling strands changed colour in a random pattern. However, it is becoming increasingly popular as a means of creating a starry night sky on the ceiling or a lit pathway underfoot, with a single light source resulting in a random scatter of individual lights.

More recently, lighting designers have played with its aesthetic potential in new and surprising ways, weaving and threading the fibres through other materials, bunching, bending and sandblasting them. Although the strands generally emit light only at the ends, they will also emit light through the coating if that is bent, and through the sides if the coating is removed. Side-emitting fibre optics can be used like very fine tubing to outline architectural shapes.

LEDs

LEDs, or light-emitting diodes, are incredibly useful tiny lights that give off hardly any heat and that last for amazingly long periods of time, between 50,000 and 100,000 hours. Giving off as much light as an incandescent bulb, they consume a fraction of the energy, a mere 3 watts.

LEDs have been in use for many decades in indicators, display panels and other forms of instrumentation – LEDs are the lights hidden away in countless products, from ovens to alarm clocks, wristwatches to cars, and the standby lights that blink away on the front of televisions and computers. Recent technological developments have meant that they are cheaper, brighter and easier to use than ever before and so they are increasingly finding their way into more practical as well as decorative lighting applications. Until the 1990s, LEDs were available only in red, orange, amber, yellow and green. The development of the blue LED and, more recently, the white, has vastly extended their creative potential.

Ingo Maurer is one designer who has made expressive use of LEDs. Aside from the 'LED Light', a witty take on the chandelier, he has also produced the 'LED Bench' (2002), where a scattering of tiny white lights, connected to a power source by near-invisible metal strips, illuminate a glass table.

Above: Requiring minimal energy and emitting very little heat, LEDs are being increasingly used in the home to great decorative effect. Here, sandwiched between fabric panels, they make a light screen/room divider.

Below: Tiny points of light illuminate individual stair treads for Hollywood-style glamour. Both LEDs and fibre optics lend themselves to the creation of starry fields of light, but they can also be used to pick out a route or to define a shape or contour.

Right: Blurring the boundary between art and lighting are designs such as this light board, which anchors small bulbs within a grid. Other similar pieces are available where the lamps are coloured.

Opposite: Ingo Maurer's 'LED Table' (2003) uses 278 tiny white LEDs to illuminate a glass table. The lights are sandwiched between two layers of laminated safety glass, emitting light on both sides. Live parts are invisible.

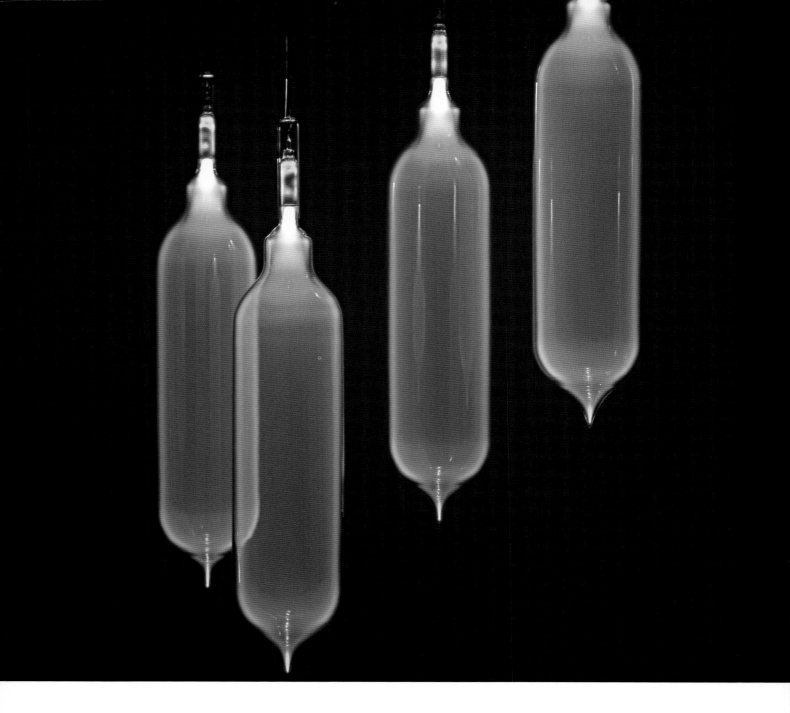

Light forms

From sculpted pendant shades to lit objects, light forms demonstrate an approach to lighting design that is often both playful in nature and of serious artistic intent. Within this category, light is the departure point for the exploration of the qualities of different materials and forms; what result can often be regarded as pieces of affordable art.

Many of these designs are deliberately left ambiguous, challenging our expectations by blurring the boundary between light and object. Others playfully assemble found materials or parts in a type of creative recycling; while some, it has to be said, definitely stray into the realms of kitsch.

Light and form also evocatively interact in the use of backlighting. Lighting fixtures, fittings or panels from within serves to dematerialize solid form. At the cutting edge of technology, fabrics are being developed that emit light themselves, where light and material are one and the same.

Sculptural designs

Practical lighting does its job, often entirely unobtrusively. With this type of decorative light, on the other hand, material and form come together to create sculptural objects that have almost as much presence when they are not illuminated as they do when they are.

One of the most famous – and most widely imitated – of all light sculptures is the 'Akari' series produced by the Japanese-American sculptor Isamu Noguchi. Noguchi was

Opposite: *Paul Cocksedge's 'Neons' are pairs of glass capsules filled with neon gas. When switched off, the glass forms are clear; when switched on, electricity flowing through the gas makes the capsules glow red.*

Inset above: *A large pendant light made of overlapping leaf shapes creates a sculptural focal point.*
Above: *These beautiful pendants suspended on long flexes are as decorative as Christmas ornaments.*

Opposite: *Kaare Klint was one of a number of Danish designers to bring an organic, sculptural quality to his work. His paper shades, which date from the 1940s and remain in production, are coated in plastic to promote longevity and make cleaning easier.*
Right: *Designed by Ferruccio Laviani for Italian manufacturers Foscarini, the 'Supernova' pendant fitting (2002) is composed of a series of parallel discs in a variety of finishes: either polished stainless steel, matt aluminium, or coloured and lacquered aluminium.*

inspired by the quality and poetic associations of light, but he was also interested in exploring light as a way of dissolving material, of making light appear to float in space.

In the early 1950s, when he was visiting Japan, Noguchi came across a group of people night-fishing on the Nagara River in Gifu City. To illuminate their work, the fishermen were using paper lanterns, or *chochin*, a traditional product of the local area; it was the sight of the lanterns bobbing over the water that inspired Noguchi to create the first of many 'Akari' designs. He had already explored light as a

medium for sculpture in his 'Lunars'; with 'Akari' he set out to create what he called 'elegant people's art'. Over half a century later, these lights are still handmade in the same way to his designs; for less than half the price of an average sofa, it is possible to own what is effectively a sculpture by an important twentieth-century artist. What distinguishes 'Akari' from the many cheap imitations that have since poured onto the market is the quality of the paper and handmaking of the originals. 'Akari' are made in the traditional way from *washi* or mulberry bark paper, which ages gracefully, glued over a

spiral hoop skeleton of springy bamboo; supports are spindly metal armatures that allow for different biomorphic forms.

The same sculptural blend of light and material can be seen in the work of many Scandinavian designers, most notably Poul Henningsen and Kaare Klint. Klint's folded and pleated paper shades and Henningsen's 'PH' series, with shades in the form of organic metal leaves, are as striking unlit as they are when switched on. A similar organic quality can be seen in the recent work of Paul Cocksedge. In his 'Styrene' shade, light is atmospherically diffused through a form made of baked polystyrene cups, drawing beauty out of what most people discard without a thought.

A rather different approach is evident in the work of Achille Castiglioni. His 'Arco' light, where a cup-like pendant is suspended at the end of an arching steel stem anchored by a block of white marble, is a contemporary icon and one of the most commercially successful modern lighting designs. However, Castiglioni's work using found or assembled pieces has had an equal, if not greater, influence on contemporary lighting designers. The 'Toio' uplighter (1965) was the product of random experimentation with items found in a garage. With a stem made from a fishing rod, a band saw as the brace and a car headlamp as the light source, 'Toio' echoes the 'ready-mades' of Duchamps and the Surrealists. Very few ready-made designs exist in the mass market; most are designed as one-offs for exhibition. An exception is 'Eight-Fifty Light' by Claire Norcross (2002), now manufactured by Habitat. This pendant light is made from plastic tags used in industrial packaging, arranged to produce a bristly sphere.

Many designers are inspired by the iconography of lighting, most particularly the potent symbol of the incandescent

Above left: *Wall panels featuring stylized lit flower shapes provide the gentlest of light in a nursery.*

Left: *A contemporary classic from noted German designer Ingo Maurer, 'Lucellino' (1992) is a bulb in flight. It is available in a variety of formats, including a table lamp and wall light. This flock of three wall lights makes a witty reference to those kitsch ornaments, the flying plaster ducks.*

Opposite top: *Superbly sculptural designs created by Nico Heilmann for* Tecnolumen in 2002, these airy, curvaceous designs are made of heat-resistant strips of plastic lamella shading a light source. The shapes recall natural forms such as pearls and shells and the lights are available as either table or pendant lamps.

Opposite below left: *'Hugging Lamp' by Gitta Gschwendtner can snuggle around a table leg.*

Opposite below right: *'Waves' by Margaret O'Rorke is a thrown porcelain lit wall sculpture.*

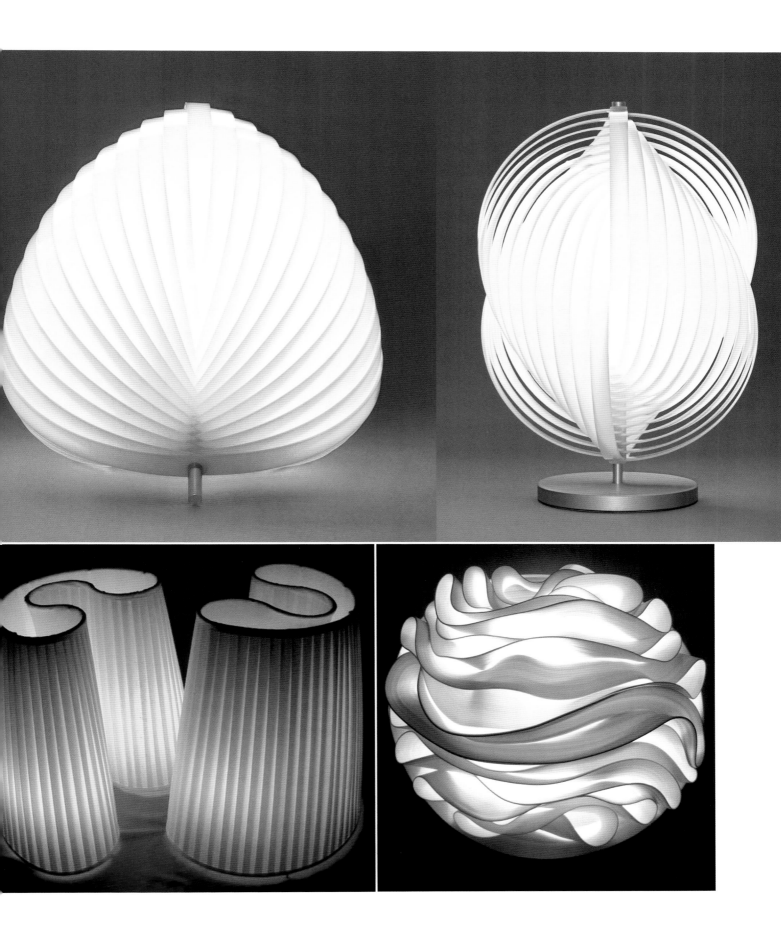

Left: *One of the 'Akari' paper lanterns from the Japanese master Noguchi, this design is part light, part spatial marker and part sculpture. Widely (and poorly) imitated, the original designs, which are still handmade today, are noted for their quality. The paper is made from mulberry bark and the shade is attached to thin springy bamboo spirals.*
Opposite: *'Rosy Angelis' (1994) by Philippe Starck represents a modern reinvention of the floor lamp. The light stands on a metal tripod and the shade is simply a veil of cotton draped over the frame.*

bulb. Ingo Maurer, a hugely influential and inventive designer, is perhaps best known for his 'Lucellino' (1992), literally a winged bulb. The design consists of a goose-feathered light bulb mounted on a pliable copper wire around which the flex is twined. The bulb can be dimmed by touching the wire. Similarly, Fontana Arte manufactures a table lamp made of porcelain where the entire lamp is the light. You can choose whether to illuminate just the base, the 'shade' or the topmost rim, or a combination of the above.

Where light and form interact in the most concrete way is in what might be termed lit objects. The classic contemporary example is Tom Dixon's 'Jack' light (1996), an overscaled jack made of polypropylene that is strong enough to sit on. A single 'Jack' light makes the point clearly enough: is it a seat that lights up or a light you can sit on? Several 'Jacks' stacked or placed on the floor readily bring to mind the reference implied by the name. Tables and chairs that light up reveal a similarly playful blurring of object and function. British

designers Totem, for example, have produced an interactive polyethylene stool. 'Boo!' comes in a range of five bright colours and has a suede top. Sit on it and it lights up.

At the cheap and cheerful end of the market, there are a host of lit objects that can bring a touch of levity to the interior. Brightly coloured illuminated dogs, pigeons that light up and glowing portable balls are just some of the designs that are available now for the young at heart.

Like chandeliers, sculptural designs, whether playful or not, naturally grab the attention. For this reason, they require prominent placing and plenty of surrounding breathing space. Many pendants fall into the category of sculptural forms; the more intriguing a pendant appears when it is switched off, the better it serves as a decorative focal point. If you are making this type of statement, however, do not proceed to fill the same space with other equally prominent fixtures. The result will either be an uncomfortable sense of distraction, with different elements clamouring for attention, or the interior will start to resemble a lighting showroom.

The same more or less applies where the light form invites a double-take. While it might be a little overwhelming to fill one's home with a collection of lighting one-liners, such tongue-in-cheek designs bring a childlike sense of delight and fun to the interior. If you can't resist collecting such pieces, a number of quirky lit objects grouped together is more effective than scattering them about from place to place.

Backlit panels

Light not only illuminates, it suggests insubstantiality, weightlessness and transparency. In this capacity, light can be used to visually dissolve solid form, so that bulky fixtures and fittings appear less dominant. This strategy has a particular application in fitted rooms such as kitchens and bathrooms, as well as in other built-in storage areas. Similarly, it can be a good way of making confined spaces appear more expansive.

Panels that are backlit need to have sufficient opacity to read as a single illuminated plane, but be transparent enough for the light to shine through. It can also be very effective if the panel is sufficiently transparent so that the contents of a cupboard or storage unit appear as a series of beguiling silhouettes. Suitable materials include frosted or etched glass and translucent Perspex, while tinted panels add the extra dimension of colour. As far as the light source is concerned, fluorescent and low-voltage halogen, which emit less heat,

Above: *Wall-hung units can look boxy and obtrusive in a kitchen. Here, lighting concealed within the cabinet makes for a much less oppressive effect, echoing the transparency of the window. Translucent front panels conceal the contents of the cupboard sufficiently to reduce visual clutter, but allow glimpses of intriguing outlines.*

Above: *Backlighting panels enclosing bathtubs and sinks can make what is often quite an enclosed fitted space feel more expansive. The glow of green light is particularly suitable for an area devoted to washing and bathing.*

Opposite: *Contemporary kitchens, with their expanses of gleaming steel and glass surfaces, can seem a little forbidding and hard-edged. This backlit glass splashback softens the material aesthetic and furnishes a welcoming glow of ambient light.*

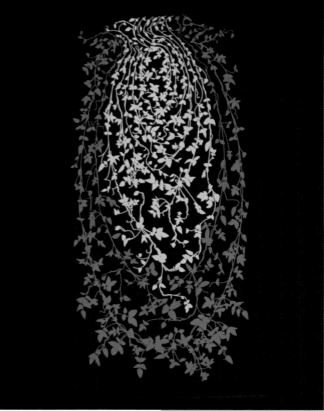

are ideal. You can use strips or tubes for an even wash of light, or individual bulbs for a more dappled effect. A single strip positioned at the top or bottom of a panel will delineate the edge with light and send a glow over the rest of the surface.

In the kitchen, many people find that wall-hung units are overly dominant and make the space appear enclosed and visually cluttered. However, in some instances they might be necessary to provide enough storage. Backlighting translucent cabinet fronts can be a very effective way of reducing their impact. The same is true of built-in wardrobes. Backlit glass or Perspex wardrobe doors provide a gentle ambient light source. In the bathroom, backlit bath panels and sink plinths introduce a sense of lightness that can go a long way towards making what may be a rather tight layout seem more spacious.

Light and fabric

Fabric has long been used as a gentle diffuser of light. Recent technological advances have seen designers creating materials that are light-emitting themselves. In the future, the increasing miniaturization of light sources and developments in materials technology may one day see the ultimate light source of all – wearable light. Today, strands of fibre optics, which can be woven, knitted or crocheted into light-emitting materials or forms, offer great scope for experiment. In another departure, Luminex, named by *Time* magazine as one of 2003's 'coolest inventions', is a new type of material where the tiny flexible fibres used in physics experiments are woven into ordinary fabric. The light-emitting fabric has been used to make curtains, clothing and handbags; power comes from a small battery.

British designer Rachel Wingfield is interested in the properties of electroluminescence to simulate the natural world. Her 'Digital Dawn' blind uses phosphorus printing ink that lights up in response to lowering light levels; the darker the room, the brighter the blind.

Above left: *A backlit wall in a hall provides a moody introduction.*
Above: *British artist/designer Rachel Wingfield has been exploring the reactive properties of electroluminescence. 'Digital Dawn' is a window blind that responds to ambient light levels. Patterned with images of plants, the blind incorporates sensors that monitor light levels and change the pattern, so that the plants appear to grow or die back as the light changes.*
Opposite: *'Light Sleeper Bedding', by Rachel Wingfield, transforms ordinary textiles into reactive light sources, with the aim of treating SAD. Research shows that exposure to early morning light is more effective at setting our body clocks when light brightens gradually, so the bedding begins to glow in a breathing rhythm over a period of 15 to 20 minutes.*

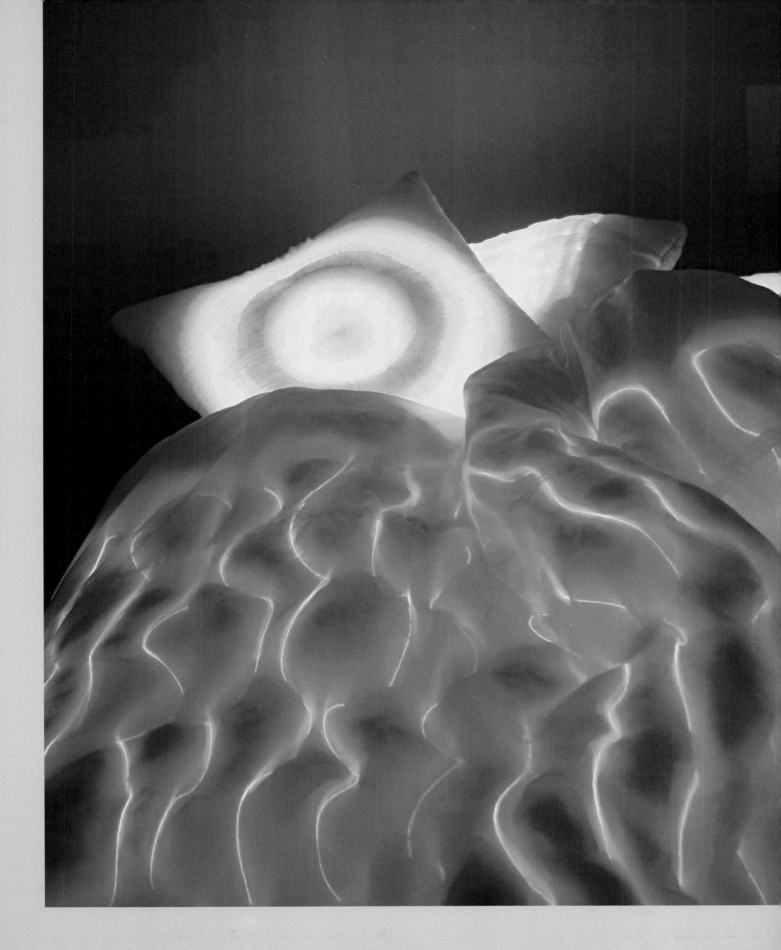

Mobile light

We tend to think of light as a steady stream of illumination, fixed at a constant level, directed at one particular place. Indoors, at night, and under artificial light sources, that may well be the case. In the daytime, however, particularly out of doors, the quality of light changes all the time, varying in intensity according to the time of day and also according to atmospheric conditions. This constant mobility may not be consciously appreciated at all times – but walk along an avenue shaded by trees and see the dappled patches of light and shade shift and change on the ground, or stroll beside the sea and see the light glinting off the water, and that entrancing quality is instantly brought home to you.

Natural light, of course, is inherently full of vitality. The celebrated Scottish architect and designer Charles Rennie Mackintosh appreciated that fact. At Hill House, one of his most famous buildings, a table he designed specifically for the house is placed in the centre of an angled south-facing bay window. As the sun moves around from one side of the bay to the other, the table, with its base of open latticework, serves as a sundial, sweeping shadows across the floor from one side of the room to the other. The great English architect Sir Edwin Lutyens was similarly attuned to the mobility of natural light. At Munstead Wood, the house he designed for his design partner Gertrude Jekyll, careful placement

of the windows in line with the house's orientation mean that the shifting patterns of light in the interior are almost as reliable as a clock when it comes to telling the time of day.

Close behind natural light in terms of mobility are fire and candlelight. The flicker of flames has an almost mesmerizing effect, and seems to be companionable, as if the light were a living thing. For artificial light to attain the same degree of mobility, it needs a helping hand. Dimmers allow you to adjust the light level, but in a rather static way. Lights with pierced shades are mobile to a degree, if positioned where they might sway a little in a through breeze. Otherwise, it is generally a case of motorized assistance. Disco balls that cast

Opposite: *Tord Boontje's 'Shadow Light' uses a small halogen bulb to project images of butterflies, squirrels and rabbits through coloured acetate. The result is to wallpaper the room in a woodland fantasia.*

Above: *Mathmos' classic retro product, the lava lamp, dates back to the early 1960s. It comes in a variety of designs and colours, including the ever-popular rocket shape.*

Overleaf: *The mirrored disco or glitter ball is an instant way of creating dance-hall glamour and glitz at home, whatever your surroundings.*

twirling bubbles of light over the walls and ceiling provide great atmosphere – for special occasions at least. More tranquillizing in effect are children's carousel lights that either make use of a motor or harness the heat generated by the light source to create beguiling patterns of moving shapes and colours. Then there is the retro classic, the lava lamp, where a concealed light source sends globules of coloured wax bubbling up through a clear glass container.

More recent developments include programmable light sequences or projections – what one might call an entirely new interpretation of 'home cinema'. Contemporary designers, such as Rachel Wingfield, have also experimented with electroluminescent technology to produce lit screens or panels that respond to movement or sound.

Firelight and candlelight

Everyone loves a fire, and everyone feels special by candlelight. On practical grounds, there is virtually no reason why these pre-electric forms of heating and lighting should have lingered on. The reason why candles are still bought and sold in their millions and why an open fireplace remains on people's wish lists when hunting for a new house is that both firelight and candlelight have a powerful allure. It's not simply a question of nostalgia, although that plays a part. Rather, it is the soothing effect of watching dancing flames in the hearth or the flicker of guttering candles that we find so irresistible.

Mobility is what firelight is all about and it is the continual movement of the flames that inspire that particularly rich sort of daydreaming most people experience when curled up beside the hearth. But there are other elements in the sensory package. The levels of light emitted by a fire or candle are much lower than most forms of artificial light, even when dimmed, which means the light is glare-free, mysterious and ultimately (if we are honest) flattering. Flattering, too, is the colour, much warmer and more golden even than tungsten, the warmest of all artificial light sources. Then there is sound – evident in the crackle of the flames themselves as much as in the shift of logs or settling of coals in the grate. A further dimension is smell. Woodsmoke is one of the most evocative domestic scents; certain species of wood give off particular aromas of their own.

Left: *A contemporary wood-burning stove has a glazed front so that you can enjoy the sight of the fire. There are many modern designs of stoves and fireplaces on the market.*
Opposite: *Antique storm lanterns suspended at varying heights over a dining table make a hospitable focus. Lanterns, both original period pieces and modern reproductions, are widely available from a variety of outlets.*

In terms of scent, candles offer a unique feel-good factor and an unbeatable way of providing a little do-it-yourself aromatherapy. There are dozens of perfumes from which to choose, from the good old-fashioned housekeeping smell of beeswax, to the relaxing scent of lavender or the spicy tang of neroli, each scent having its own impact on mood and ambience. There are few better ways to relax than in a hot tub with a few scented candles burning near by.

Fireplaces are natural focal points and they tend to take pride of place in living areas. Where modern houses have a fireplace – and many still do – the living room is where it will generally be located. If you live in a period house, fireplaces elsewhere may have been removed and the hearths blocked up. It may well be worth reinstating a fireplace, provided you do not need the additional wall area that it will occupy in order to make furniture arrangement work. A small hearth in a bedroom adds a cosy sense of intimacy; while

an open fire in a bathroom is the height of indulgence and sensuousness. Reproduction fire surrounds are widely available, although original examples are not difficult to find in salvage yards and from specialist antique fireplace suppliers. If you are unsure about which style and material would be appropriate for your house, neighbouring properties may have existing fireplaces that you can study. In Victorian houses, for example, bedroom fireplaces tended to be made of cast iron with tiled surrounds; stone and marble surrounds are more common in larger public rooms.

In addition to period or reclaimed fireplaces, there are also a number of stunning contemporary designs. When buying or commissioning a new fireplace, you do not need to restrict yourself to wall sites. Modern designs with their cylindrical flues can look good in the centre of a space, particularly in open-plan areas; you can also have double-sided fireplaces, which serve as spatial dividers. Many of these

contemporary designs are fairly minimal, which throws the focus of attention right onto the fire itself. Wood- or solid fuel-burning stoves are another alternative; while simulated fires, where the flames are fed by a gas jet rather than lit fuel, have vastly improved in looks in recent years and they are no longer the tacky option they once were. Whichever design you choose, you will need expert installation.

Candles need no such forethought or commitment to fixed arrangement. For an instant sense of occasion, even a collection of tealights lined up down the table or along a mantelpiece will do the job. Aside from scented varieties, there are many different types of candles on the market, plain or coloured; tapering, square, round or stubby; expensive and hand-dipped; cheap and cheerful. Flares make unbeatable garden lighting, spiked into the ground beside paths.

Candleholders, too, ring the changes from period-style candelabra to modern sculptural designs. You can also buy glass or metal candle sconces to hang on the wall or suspend candles in individual glass jars or pierced metal lanterns. Then, of course, many chandeliers, both period and modern, are designed to be lit by candles rather than candle bulbs. Flickering flames are appealing, but not if the candles keep blowing out. Storm lanterns and other glass shields are particularly useful when burning candles out of doors.

Because we are not as accustomed to these living light sources as, perhaps, our grandparents were, it is particularly important always to keep safety in mind. Never leave candles burning for more than a minute or so in an empty room. Never leave children unsupervised near naked flames of any kind. Fireplaces should be regularly inspected and chimneys swept out to make sure poisonous gases are not leaking through cracked flue linings. Always use a fireguard or screen.

Light projections

Light projections can provide the ultimate sensurround experience. Contemporary bars and hotels have been experimenting with such cinematic lighting effects for some time; nowadays, sophisticated control systems are available so that you can enjoy the same type of spectacle at home.

A projection can be as straightforward as a slide show on a patch of white wall. At the opposite extreme, programmable systems enable you to vary colours, intensity and patterns according to mood. Such systems (and the professional lighting advice you will require from a consultant) are not cheap, but with light playing such a starry role in the interior, who needs to splash out on an expensive sofa?

Light and water

In light and water, two powerful feel-good factors come together. Swimming in the sea under a clear blue sky, sunlight glinting off the water, or swimming in an indoor pool, ripples of light glancing off the ceiling, are entrancing experiences.

In the home, however, light and water have a problem. Water and electricity are lethal in combination, which rules out certain types of light fitting for bathroom and shower use, especially those where the bulb or metal parts are exposed to the risk of splashing. Low-voltage (12V) light sources are recommended over mains fittings.

Recessed fittings can make good practical sense in bathrooms and showers because of the fixed nature of the layout. A greater number of relatively dim lights is better than a few brighter ones and will reduce the risk of glare, particularly as in the bathroom surfaces and finishes tend to be glossy and reflective. Many shower enclosures come with their own array of built-in lights; otherwise there are a number of sealed and waterproof fittings from which to choose, from tiny recessed spotlights to surface-mounted bulkhead fittings. If at all possible, try to arrange bathroom and shower lighting so that it is dimmable.

Fibre optics brings a special magic to bathroom lighting. Because the light source is remotely located, there is no risk whatsoever of water coming in contact with electricity.

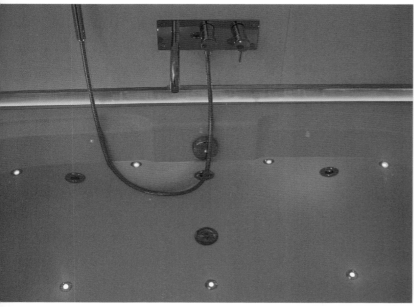

Opposite far left: *This spa bath features a number of LED ports set into the inner skin of the tub. Other models include chromatherapy baths where sequences of different colours wash the water with light.*

Above and left: *Water and light are magical companions. The safest way of exploiting the visual dynamic is with fibre optics. Here, a standard showerhead is surrounded by a constellation of tiny points of light. The plywood ceiling was drilled with holes through which the individual strands of fibre optics were fed. Because the light source is a light box that is sited remotely, there is no risk that water can come in contact with electricity.*

Taps (faucets) and showerheads lit by fibre optics transform bathing and showering into a theatrical experience, with droplets catching the light like so many tiny crystals. While the kit is quite expensive, the effect is unforgettable and is particularly evocative in wet rooms and minimalist bathrooms.

Manufacturers of up-market bathroom fittings produce bathtubs with integral lighting. These tiny points of light make the water glow in a soothing and restful way; there are often colour settings, too. Another evocative form of lighting is special tiles inset with LEDs. Fully waterproof and consuming only 1 watt of energy, these tiles can be used on the floor, ceiling or walls and have a life of 50,000 hours (or 15 years).

Lighting pools, ponds and water features out of doors has great decorative impact. There are practical advantages, too. A lit pool is not only a glowing focal point, it is also a far safer place in which to swim on warm summer nights. Many swimming pool manufacturers and suppliers produce integral lights for swimming pools, which often take the form of bulkhead or recessed fittings. These can be combined with low-level lights placed around the edge of the pool to graze the ground or paving with light. Avoid placing fittings higher up, which will create an unacceptable light spill that might disturb neighbours or contribute to light pollution.

Lighting for purely decorative water features should also be relatively dim and positioned at low level. Moving jets of water look dramatic when directly lit, but training light at a standing pond can make it look flat and murky. The answer is to bounce light from an adjacent wall or similar surface.

Simplest of all ways in which to combine light with water are floating candles and nightlights. Bobbing on the surface of the water – whether it's a tub or a garden pool – they are an inexpensive way of creating impromptu decorative effects.

Above left and left: 'A Lamp in My Swimming Pool' (2003), designed by Héctor Serrano for Spanish manufacturer Metalarte, features a floating base adapted from emergency lifebuoy lights attached to a waterproof lampshade. The white LEDs that comprise the light source are battery-powered and rechargeable; the light lasts for six hours at a time. To turn off the light, you turn it upside down.

Opposite: More conventionally, swimming pools are generally lit with special fittings that are either recessed into the pool walls or surface-mounted. Underwater lighting illuminates the water; fibre optics can also be used to light the rim of the pool.

Light and colour

Colour has a direct line to the subconscious. Depending on the particular shade, it can be stimulating or sedating, uplifting or soothing; along with such emotional effects go a host of cultural meanings and associations. In combination with light, the impact of colour in the interior is hugely enhanced. Ranging from basic diffusion to the very latest programmable systems of colourwashing, there are many different ways in which light can work in creative partnership with colour.

Colour and mood

Colour itself is a function of the way we see light. Natural light is radiant energy that travels to us from the sun on different wavelengths, with each wavelength corresponding to a different colour in the spectrum. The reason grass looks green is because it has absorbed all the wavelengths of light except green, which it then reflects back to our eyes.

Each colour has a wavelength and each wavelength requires a different adjustment of eye and brain. During the day the wavelengths in the middle of the spectrum, which correspond to the the colour green, are the easiest to see, which is why green landscapes are so restful and green-tinted blinds and glass have long been considered good for the eyes. The long wavelengths that correspond to the colour red, on the other hand, demand maximum adjustment, which is why the colour seems physically to leap out at us. That stimulus, in turn, is interpreted as excitement, alarm or arousal. Our emotional responses to different colours are fundamentally derived from such physical causes and changes.

While we all know colour affects the way we feel, some people believe that it can also have a role in healing. In chromatherapy, coloured light is used to correct imbalances in the body's energy centres, which practitioners believe could cause illnesses and disorders. The cool colours of the spectrum – violet, indigo and blue – which are calming and soothing, are used for combating stress and sleeping disorders. The warm colours – yellow, orange and red – which are stimulating, are used to alleviate tiredness and give a boost to creativity and concentration. Green, the balancing shade in the middle of the spectrum, is thought to be good for trauma. Colour therapy is generally administered with

Above: *Fluorescent tubes are available in a range of colours, ideal for decorative lighting effects. Unlike neon, fluorescent tubes require no specialist installation and can be run off normal mains voltage. In addition, they are very energy-efficient and long-lasting.*

Opposite: *A vibrant display of colour has been achieved by covering a series of 'mini link' fluorescent tubes with sheets of intensely coloured gel.*

light boxes and coloured filters. A related development is shower cubicles, bathtubs and sinks fitted with LEDs so that the showerer or bather is washed by a succession of colours. The lights can be preset to a single colour or programmed to change colours in sequence.

Diffusion

Shining light through a translucent coloured material is one of the most basic ways of combining light with colour. Rose-tinted card or silk shades create a warm and flattering light; shades incorporating pieces of coloured glass, such as Louis Comfort Tiffany's Art Nouveau designs, have the same jewel-like intensity as stained-glass windows. A tube or rope light diffused behind a panel of coloured glass or Perspex has a more architectural effect.

Coloured bulbs operate in much the same way. In this case, it is not the light source that is responsible for the colour but the coloured glass envelope that surrounds it. Coloured bulbs range from those that are tinted to warm up the light just a little bit to gaudier, more vibrant examples whose application, outside clubs and bars, is perhaps rather more limited.

Above: *At St Martin's Lane Hotel in London, designed by Philippe Starck, bedrooms feature interactive colourwashing programmes so that guests can choose between different ambiences and moods. The basic décor of the bedrooms is pure white to maximize the intensity of the colour effects.*

Coloured light

In comparison to natural light, in which all colours combine to form white, all artificial sources are coloured to some degree. While halogen approaches the pure white of natural light, tungsten has a definite yellowish cast and standard fluorescent is greenish. In most situations, however, our eyes correct the light from such sources so that we read it as white.

Coloured light, that is, light produced from a light source rather than diffused through a coloured bulb, includes LEDs, coloured fluorescent and neon. As previously mentioned, the advantage of LEDs is that they are very energy-efficient and long-lasting. While they cost more, the initial investment is repaid over time. Ceiling-mounted clusters of LEDs can be set to change through red, green and blue, or programmed so that all colours shine simultaneously, giving the effect of white light. Neon, the familiar lighting of commercial signage, produces very intensely coloured light, but requires high voltages and specialist installation. Much more user-friendly are fluorescent tubes. The colour range is vast, the price affordable and no special installation is required. Coloured fluorescent tubes can be concealed behind baffles or in recesses to give a defining line, or mounted behind glass or Perspex for a more diffusing glow.

Left: 'Microchrome', designed by Jeremy Lord, is a light artwork that uses LEDs. Lord, who says he 'makes lights to look at, not read a book by', produces a number of limited edition wall-hanging artworks that explore sequences of light and colour.

Below: Colour is an element that is exploited in many light boxes and light boards. Some of these are produced commercially as products; others are one-off pieces created by lighting artists.

Left and above: *Colour has a huge impact on our emotions. It can make us feel uplifted and energized, or tranquil and relaxed. Conventional décor, reliant on paint, furnishings and fixed surfaces and materials, is a static way of experiencing colour; if you feel like a change, you have to redecorate. Coloured lighting, on the other hand, allows you to change the atmosphere instantly, according to your mood, the time of day, the season, the light levels or any other factor. Here, a kitchen is transformed from a warm, rosy intimate space to one that is cool-toned and expansive at the touch of a switch.*

Colourwashing

The ultimate way to combine light with colour is to invest in a colourwashing lighting system. Early examples featured in designer hotels, notably St Martin's Lane in London, designed by Philippe Starck, where interactive coloured lighting in the rooms allowed guests to set their own mood. Similar systems are available for home lighting schemes; the cost to light a living area is about half the price of an average sofa.

Colourwashing bathes areas in coloured light. Operated remotely, most systems offer a variety of effects and a vast range of shades: you can set the system to change in a rolling sequence at a given rate. For greatest impact, light needs to be directed at a white wall. Glossy white floors and reflective or transparent surfaces such as glass multiply the effect.

Opposite: *Coloured light has a certain irreverence and frivolity about it. Here, it adds a vibrant and light-hearted accent to a sleek modern kitchen with stainless-steel worktops and built-in units. Two light boxes, which serve as supports to the extended countertop, glow shocking pink.*
Below: *A row of pierced-metal light boxes bathe an empty corridor in warm yellow light.*

the com

From exuberant decorative designs to discreet concealed fixtures, the choice has never been greater when it comes to light fittings. This section offers a selection of the type of products that are currently available in every category of fitting, including some contemporary classics from designers such as Castiglioni, Starck and Henningsen. There is also detailed information on different light sources, switches and controls, and essential practical information concerning installation, energy-saving strategies and safety.

Light fittings

Uplighters, downlights, spotlights and track fittings

Uplighters, downlights, spotlights and track fittings are invaluable both for creating a gentle glow of background light, bounced off the planes of walls and ceilings, and for more focused illumination, either to pick out decorative displays and points of interest, or to boost light levels in working areas, such as kitchen countertops. When choosing any type of light fitting, it is important to assess the quality of light it produces, rather than simply base your selection on the appearance of the fitting itself. You need to establish before you buy it that the spread of light suits your particular requirements and that the fitting can be adjusted to target light where you are going to need it.

Many of these fittings are deliberately discreet, with the emphasis on the function they perform rather than decorative elements. Most self-effacing of all, perhaps, are the recessed downlights that fit flush with the ceiling. Installing fixed lights, such as downlights, track lights and spot lights, is generally a job for a professional.

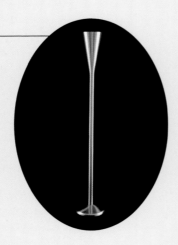

Luminator, designed by Pietro Chiesa in 1933, is a sleek floor-standing uplighter where the light source is completely concealed within the attentuated conical reflector and integral stem. It is available in nickel-plated brass or aluminium painted with an anti-reflective finish. The light source is halogen and is dimmable.
Manufacturer/outlet: *Fontana Arte*

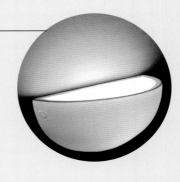

Wall-mounted uplighters are widely available in ceramic or plaster and can be painted in with the wall decoration. This design, by ceramicist Lucy Bilcock, is made of porcelain, a material that diffuses the light and gives it a warm, intimate glow. Most of the light, however, is directed upwards and reflects off the wall.
Manufacturer/outlet: *Diffuse*

Kedy spotlight, from Habitat, is a neat and unobtrusive design that is ideal for producing targeted, focused light in many areas of the home. This halogen spot is fully adjustable. The base is made of brushed aluminium.
Manufacturer/outlet: *Habitat*

Luxmaster F floor lamp, designed by Jasper Morrison, is a halogen light that can be positioned at any height on the supporting steel pole and rotated through 360 degrees to serve as an uplight or downlight or to reflect light from the wall. Transparent electrical wire is wound around the rod.
Manufacturer/outlet: *Flos*

Tenso, designed by Franco Bettonica and Mario Melocchi in 1998, is a lighting system that can be used to create a variety of effects, both diffused and directional. The track can be mounted horizontally, vertically or diagonally and is ideal for rooms with very high ceilings, vaults, arches or beams.
Manufacturer/outlet: *Cini & Nils*

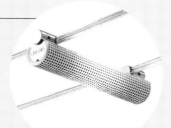

A track fitting from Habitat, this wall-mounted system suspends five individual lights from cabling. Diffused through white porcelain shades, the light is soft and semi-directional. This type of fitting would provide a gentle source of illumination for a dining table.
Manufacturer/outlet: *Habitat*

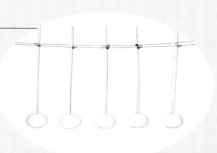

A variant of the Tenso system above, **miniTensoTeli** is a cable-mounted plug-in halogen luminaire made of polycarbonate, metal alloy and heat-resistant glass. Used in combination with a diffuser, the effect is one of soft indirect light. It does not require a transformer.
Manufacturer/outlet: *Cini & Nils*

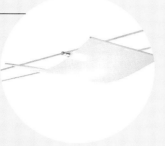

Tangent is another Habitat design. These mains-voltage halogen spots are fully adjustable and are mounted on a metal bar. The design is also available as a single spot. Targeted to bounce light off walls, such fittings provide a better quality of background light than a single central source.
Manufacturer/outlet: *Habitat*

Fari is a range of small high-powered luminaires specifically designed for accent lighting. Each fitting can be oriented individually in every direction. The lights come in floor, wall-mounted, ceiling and track versions. The spots do not require a transformer.
Manufacturer/outlet: *Cini & Nils*

Leding lighting track from IKEA consists of three adjustable halogen spotlights mounted on a curved wand of silver-coloured steel. There are many good-looking track fittings available in the mass market at affordable prices.
Manufacturer/outlet: *IKEA*

Alba is one of a range of designs that combines a low-voltage halogen downlight with a suspended crystal décor element. Downlights can be rather banal and flat in their effect. In this case, the suspended crystal plaque makes beautiful reflected patterns on the ceiling for added vitality.
Manufacturer/outlet: *Swarovski*

Faro a Barra consists of two or three parabolic spotlights suspended from a zinc-coloured painted metal rod. Different light sources – halogen, incandescent and energy-saving – can be used with this design. The spotlights swivel in every direction.
Manufacturer/outlet: *Pallucco*

fittings

Task lights and wall lights

Task lights, as the term suggests, play a supportive role in areas where concentrated work is carried out. While retro or period-style desk lamps are still widely available in the market today, many of these are more decorative than functional. Contemporary designs, articulated, counterweighted and easily positioned, provide a more practical solution.

Wall lights are an effective way of achieving discreet background light and are much less dominant than central fixtures. Many designs look best used in pairs and arranged symmetrically, in flanking alcoves, for example, or to either side of a sofa or side table. Wall lights may be omnidirectional or cast their light principally in a single direction.

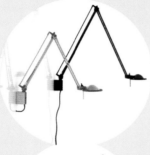

Berenice, designed by Alberto Meda and Paolo Rizzatto in 1986, and shown here in two versions, wall-mounted and freestanding, is an elegant task light with an articulated, attentuated arm made from dye-cast aluminium. The halogen light source is diffused by a coloured shade.
Manufacturer/outlet: *Luceplan*

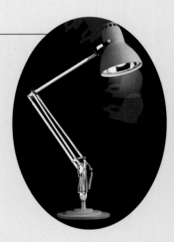

Anglepoise, designed by Kenneth Grange, is a subtle update of the original classic design by George Carwardine, first produced in the early 1930s. Carwardine was an automotive engineer and he based his revolutionary design on the anatomy of the human arm.
Manufacturer/outlet: *Anglepoise*

Archimoon Eco, by Philippe Starck, features a white powder-coated aluminium asymmetric shade with a polycarbonate cover. The base is weighted and the articulated sprung arm can be repositioned at the touch of a finger. This design is also available as a wall fitting and with a desk clamp instead of a base.
Manufacturer/outlet: *Flos*

Kelvin T table lamp, designed by Antonio Citterio, comes in different versions: with an upright angled stem, a sloping stem and an adjustable arm. The adjustable version can be extended to near-horizontal without tipping over.
Manufacturer/outlet: *Flos*

Period-style wall lights often echo earlier forms of fixture, such as sconces originally designed to take candles. This refined example features a brass swivel arm and a knife-pleated silk shade.
Manufacturer/outlet: *Vaughan*

Urka, designed by Alessandro Piva, consists of a wall-mounted galvanized metal frame. Light is diffused through a latticed screen at the front and sides and it also spills out at the top and bottom through opal acrylic.
Manufacturer/outlet: *Fontana Arte*

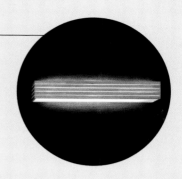

Designed in 1933, this shaded wall light still looks strikingly contemporary. The chrome arms support a pair of blue glass shades. This is the type of design that would look best used in pairs and positioned symmetrically.
Manufacturer/outlet: *Fontana Arte*

O Sole Mio, designed by Rodolfo Dordoni, is a wall light designed for bathroom use. The mirror is surrounded by a continuous illuminated strip lit by a concealed bulb to provide even lighting across the face. The design comes in two colours: blue and orange.
Manufacturer/outlet: *Flos*

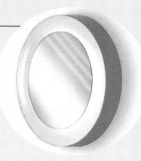

Seina wall light by Seppo Koho is a Finnish design with a Scandinavian modern aesthetic. The light is beautifully filtered through strips of natural birch. The same design is available as a pendant, floor lamp and table lamp. The wall-mounted version can be fixed either way up to direct light upwards or down.
Manufacturer/outlet: *Secto*

Riga, designed by Paolo Zani in 1995, is an elegant contemporary wall light where light is diffused through tempered and sand-blasted glass. The fitting comes in different lengths and finishes.
Manufacturer/outlet: *Fontana Arte*

Hector Pleat table lamp, designed by Peter Bowles, is a small traditional-style desk lamp with a shade made of bone china, which gives a soft diffuse light. The shade can be angled and the flex is covered with woven fabric.
Manufacturer/outlet: *Original BTC*

Isolde, designed by Matilde Alessandro in 2000, was originally produced as an installation but is now in production as a wall and ceiling fitting. Light from a 13-watt fluorescent tube is diffused through Plexiglass. It is produced in pale blue, red and off-white, with other colours available to order.
Manufacturer/outlet: *LIGHT*

Table lamps

Versatile, portable, decorative – even sculptural – the table lamp plays a key role in home lighting. In practical terms, its key asset is its ability to provide light almost anywhere you need it – beside a chair, by the bed, on a sideboard, table or desktop – requiring only a socket near by for the plug. Distinguished from the task light by the fact that the light it emits is generally diffused and omnidirectional, rather than targeted or focused on a specific area, the table lamp is inherently intimate and gentle in effect.

Traditional table lamps comprise a separate base and fabric- or paper-covered shade, with the focus of attention often falling on the base. Many contemporary designs show a departure from this pattern, with either the shade and base integrated in some fashion, or the lamp taking the form of a sculptural object. Many table lamps, both traditional and modern, come in a range of sizes so that you can suit the scale of the lamp to its setting. It is also common for lamps to be available in both floor-standing and table versions.

Part of the McCloud range of home furnishings designed by Kevin McCloud for Debenhams, a leading British department store, these table lamps with their curvaceous bases bring high style to the high street. The glossy metallic bases and narrow shades have a retro feel. Manufacturer/outlet: *Debenhams*

Fontana, designed by Max Ingrand in 1954, is a witty, evocative take on the classic table lamp. The base and shade are both made of white, satined blown glass. Bulbs concealed within the lamp can be switched so that the base, shade or shade rim light up individually or all together. Manufacturer/outlet: *Fontana Arte*

WG 24, designed by Wilhelm Wagenfeld in 1923–4, reveals the industrial aesthetic of its Bauhaus origins. The shade is opalescent glass; the stem and base are clear glass, with wiring routed through steel tubing. Eighty years after it was first designed and produced, the lamp still looks modern today. Manufacturer/outlet: *Tecnolumen*

Bourgie, designed by Ferruccio Laviani, reworks the classic table lamp into a glittering ultra-glamorous decorative object through the use of a thoroughly modern material. The entire lamp, including the shade and Baroque-style base is made of Perspex. It is available in transparent or black. Manufacturer/outlet: *Kartell*

Bague, designed by Patricia Urquiloa/Eliana Gerotto in 2003, is an elegant and beautifully detailed lamp made of perforated metal net covered with silicon resin, with a satin screen diffuser. In both material and form, the design has a sophisticated contemporary edge – this is lighting as equipment. It is available in three sizes. Manufacturer/outlet: *Foscarini*

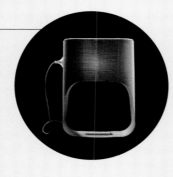

Panthella, designed by Verner Panton in 1970, is a sleek futuristic lamp whose shade is made of acrylic. Like many classic table lamps, this design is also available in a floor-standing version. Although Panton was a Danish designer, his 'pop' forms and use of synthetic materials represent a departure from the more naturalistic Scandinavian aesthetic. Manufacturer/outlet: *Louis Poulsen*

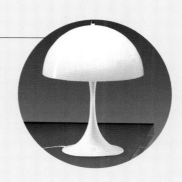

Bolla, designed by Harry and Camilla, is a study in contrasts, the thin nickel-polished brass stem supporting a globular opal white or transparent blown glass shade. Manufacturer/outlet: *Fontana Arte*

PH table lamp, designed by Poul Henningsen, is one of a series of lights, including pendants, whose design dates from the 1920s. The overlapping metal planes of the shade, made of aluminium painted white, are designed to diffuse the light and avoid glare. The organic form is very typical of modern Scandinavian design. Manufacturer/outlet: *Louis Poulsen*

A decorative design that is clearly influenced by traditional forms but that nevertheless retains a contemporary feel, this Italian table lamp features a handmade cast-iron base embellished with drops of Murano glass. Shades may be fabric- or raffia-covered. Manufacturer/outlet: *Baga*

Miss K2, designed by Philippe Starck, has a fully transparent base and a polycarbonate shade, opaline on the interior and transparent on the exterior. It provides soft diffused light and is dimmable. Manufacturer/outlet: *Flos*

Lantern, a beautifully minimal design for a table lamp by Marc Krusin, features an expressive blend of material and form, with the light source softly diffused through a cylinder of opalescent glass, bordered by narrow bands of transparent glass. As much a light wand as a lantern, it has the effect of hovering light. Manufacturer/outlet: *Fontana Arte*

Charms by Daniela Puppa features a dimpled glass diffuser, coloured above and opaque white below, mounted on a polished aluminium stem. The shade or diffuser is completely enclosed for glare-free light. The sculptural form is both playful and contemporary. Manufacturer/outlet: *Fontana Arte*

Floor lamps

Like table lamps, the floor lamp is a flexible, portable and versatile way of lighting a room; in fact, many table lamps also come in floor-standing versions. The traditional standard lamp was a mainstay of home furnishing for decades until it was supplanted by spotlights, downlights and other forms of fixed or recessed lighting. Nevertheless, there have always been more modernistic interpretations of the basic form on the market and in recent years a range of new designs that are as sculptural as they are effective have brought renewed popularity to this familiar category of fitting.

The shaded standard lamp, like the table lamp, emits light more or less in an omnidirectional fashion. While many contemporary designs follow suit, others direct light either chiefly upwards or in a more targeted fashion. Some floor lamps emit light the entire length of the fitting, which enhances their natural role as spatial markers. Positioned around the room, floor lamps deliver welcome local light to seating arrangements and, in combination with table lamps, help to provide a varied skyline.

Sag, designed by Carlo Tamborini in 2001, is rather suggestive of a traffic light. The metal frame is made out of painted aluminium and comes in three finishes: blue, red and metallic. Light from six balloon-shaped bulbs is diffused through circular cutouts.
Manufacturer/outlet: *Fontana Arte*

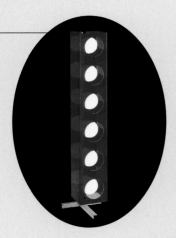

Arco is an icon of modern design created by Achille and Pier Giacomo Castiglioni in 1962. The arching stem of the light is made of stainless steel, while the shade is made of polished aluminium. The base that supports the light is a block of white marble. Arco can be adjusted to different heights and was originally designed to light a dining table.
Manufacturer/outlet: *Flos*

Toio, another example of the creative partnership between the Castiglioni brothers, Achille and Pier Giacomo, is a light fitting conceived from ready-made objects. In the 1965 original, the base was a band saw, the stem a fishing rod and a halogen car headlamp the light source.
Manufacturer/outlet: *Flos*

Lotus, designed by Janne Kyttanen and Jiri Evenhuis, using stereo lithography, a rapid prototyping technique, is a delicate-looking lotus flower made of epoxy on a slender metal stem. Light is diffused through the petals. Two colours are available, brown and orange.
Manufacturer/outlet: *Materialise*

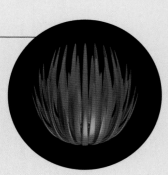

Rosy Angelis, designed by Philippe Starck, is a witty subversion of the traditional standard lamp. A spindly metal tripod and frame supporting a shade made of draped cotton fabric reduces the floor lamp to its most basic parts while retaining an element of mystery. Manufacturer/outlet: *Flos*

Spun Light F, designed by Sebastian Wrong in 2003, is a glossy, chic design whose stem almost has the appearance of poured oil or liquid. It is also available in a table lamp version. Manufacturer/outlet: *Flos*

Fortuny, designed in 1907 by Mario Fortuny y Madrazo, is an overscaled photographer's light with a steel support tripod, metal reflector and cotton diffuser. Fortuny, who was best known for his pleated silk dresses that were fashionable in the 1920s, began his career in photography. Manufacturer/outlet: *Pallucco*

XXL, designed by Antonio Citterio in 2000, consists of a square steel base and steel stem supporting a double-skinned bowl-shaped diffuser composed of glass and blown glass. Manufacturer/outlet: *Flos*

Lu-lu, designed by Stefano Casciani in 1996, is an elegant floor lamp that features a brushed-metal base, chromium-plated metal stand and diffuser made of Murano glass. The light can be switched so that either just the top is illuminated or both sections of the diffuser. Manufacturer/outlet: *Oluce*

Glo-ball, designed by Jasper Morrison in 1998, consists of a large globe made of etched glass supported by a metal base. Simplicity itself, the lamp has an endearing, almost childlike quality. The design is available in different versions: as a table lamp, pendant, and two heights of floor lamp. Manufacturer/outlet: *Flos*

Standard Floor Lamp, designed by Yosuke Watanabe for Habitat, is a clever twist on the traditional standard lamp. The design, where the 'light' is an illuminated silhouette, cut out of plastic, has gentle fun at the expense of an unfashionable object. Manufacturer/outlet: *Habitat*

AJ Visor, designed by Arne Jacobsen in 1956, is a contemporary classic. The sharp angle of the shade shields the eyes from the light source, like a visor. The stem is slightly inclined and the base has a circular cutout. This design is available in a range of colours and finishes and also comes in a table lamp version. Manufacturer/outlet: *Louis Poulsen*

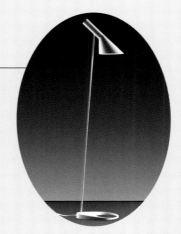

Pendant lights

The hanging or pendant fixture provides intimate ambient lighting for the dining table and a decorative focus of interest for living areas. Provided such fittings are not the sole source of light in a given area, they can be a very effective way of generating background light, in tandem with others that reflect light from the walls and ceiling. Pendants often look good hung in groups or pairs rather than singly, and at staggered heights. A series of pendants can be used to light the length of a dining table: the key is to fix them at a height that does not cause glare, nor interfere with views across the table.

The paper lantern is probably one of the most popular pendants of all time. While it is cheap and effective at diffusing light in a soft and gentle way, it is so ubiquitous that it scarcely registers. Recently, designers have turned their attention to the pendant form and come up with a range of innovative products in different, often unexpected, materials.

Crosslight is a double-cruciform light that is available as a pendant, floor lamp or table lamp, or as part of a chandelier ensemble. It comes in white and orange; the white version produces a soft ambient glow, while the orange emits both a warm diffused colour and reflects small white globes on surrounding surfaces.
Manufacturer/outlet: *Dutchbydesign*

0024, designed by celebrated Italian designer Gio Ponti in 1931, features a chrome-plated brass frame supporting concentric transparent glass discs. The central diffuser, which conceals a tube bulb, is made of sandblasted glass. From the side, the fitting almost appears to dematerialize.
Manufacturer/outlet: *Fontana Arte*

Fuchsia, designed by Achille Castiglioni, diffuses the light from the bulb through a conical hand-blown glass shade with a sandblasted edge that glows in the light. This type of design looks good hung in a series along the length of a table or counter.
Manufacturer/outlet: *Flos*

Huna, which dates from 1965, is a high-tech industrial-style fitting of the type commonly used to furnish lofts and converted warehouses. The shade is made of aluminium and is available either in a natural finish, or painted white, black or forest green.
Manufacturer/outlet: *Fontana Arte*

Romeo Moon, designed by Philippe Starck, is a pendant light that provides diffused light through a double-skinned shade consisting of an inner diffuser of acid-etched glass and an outer layer of pressed clear glass. The fixture, which is relatively heavy, is supported on steel cables. Manufacturer/outlet: *Flos*

Bigoli, designed by Phay Halsackda in 2003, consists of a mass of springy spirals and twists of tubular mesh that surround the light source. Most commonly seen as a pendant, the shade can also be used with a stand as a floor lamp. Manufacturer/outlet: *Innermost*

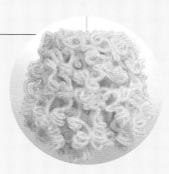

Styrene, designed by Paul Cocksedge, is a shade made from white polystyrene cups that are baked and then stuck together to create an organic form that softly diffuses light. Shades are made to order by the designer. Manufacturer/outlet: *Paul Cocksedge*

Midsummer light, designed by Tord Boontje in 2004, is a double-layer paper pendant wrapped around a cone-shaped protector to prevent the shade coming in direct contact with the light source. It comes in five colours: white, blue, red/yellow, green/yellow and fuchsia/pink. The paper is the unrippable type used to make security envelopes. Manufacturer/outlet: *Dutchbydesign*

Eight-Fifty light, designed by Claire Norcross in 2002, is a spiky sphere composed of plastic tags that are used in industrial packaging. The lights used to be made by hand by the designer, who began her career in textiles, but are now in commercial production. Manufacturer/outlet: *Habitat*

Artichoke light, designed by Poul Henningsen in the 1920s, is an icon of Scandinavian modern design. The overlapping steel planes that give the design its name have a natural, organic quality and create a beautiful diffusion of light. Manufacturer: *Louis Poulsen*

Klint shade, one of series designed by Kaare Klint from the mid-1940s onwards, is a sculptural fitting in folded and pleated plastic or plastic-coated paper. Most of these shades are still hand-assembled. Manufacturer/outlet: *Le Klint*

Icon pendant, designed by Ferruccio Laviani in 2003, is almost 60cm (2ft) in diameter. Playful in its reference to pop culture, the shade is made from colour-tinted transparent vinyl that reduces the glare from the visible bulb but also remains slightly iridescent. Manufacturer/outlet: *Kartell*

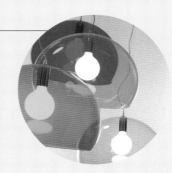

Chandeliers

Until fairly recently, the chandelier was notable in its absence from design-conscious homes. Too over-the-top for minimalist surroundings, and too much associated with period style to sit easily in a contemporary interior, it fell out of favour for a considerable time. All this has changed in the past few years, and the chandelier is once more a highly desirable object. In clean-lined and otherwise understated rooms, it provides a welcome touch of theatricality, while in period settings it remains as much at home as it ever was. In either case, the chandelier is a considerable focal point and requires plenty of breathing space to be displayed to its best advantage. Some designs are significantly heavy.

Traditional chandeliers have never gone out of production and there is a wide range from which to choose, including relatively inexpensive repro models, reclaimed or salvaged period pieces and handmade confections in glass and lead crystal. At the same time, contemporary designers have increasingly turned their attention to the chandelier and have reinterpreted it in inventive and often witty ways.

Wineglass chandelier is an example of the playful approach that the chandelier often inspires. This cascading design, the product of a collaboration between Gitta Gschwendtner and Carl Clerkin, is available as a kit of 18 wine glasses that you clip upside down around a light source onto nylon threads. Manufacturer/outlet: *2pm*

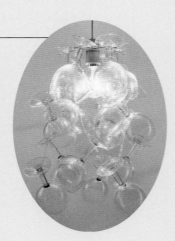

Sarfatti pendant, designed by Gino Sarfatti in 1958, is a modernist interpretation of the chandelier, featuring 30 unshaded bulbs on a branched chrome-plated fitting. The chandelier can be displayed with a drop of 3m (10ft). Manufacturer/outlet: *Flos*

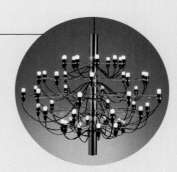

Devonshire pendant is an electrified chandelier fitted with unshaded opaque candle bulbs. The painted metal armature is prettily decorated with glass drops and ropes of glass beads. Manufacturer/outlet: *Jim Lawrence*

Fun, the creation of pop designer Verner Panton in 1977, hovers on the boundary between pendant shade and chandelier. Suspended from the metal tiered rings are mother-of-pearl seashells that tinkle in the breeze. The design is still made in Denmark. Manufacturer/outlet: *Aspects*

I Spy is another ironic take on tradition. This chandelier is composed of descending tiers of plastic magnifying glasses, which fracture the light in the same intriguing way as crystal, although in a far less pricey fashion. Manufacturer/outlet: *Habitat*

Garland, designed by Tord Boontje, is the mass-market version of the 'Wednesday Light' and was a runaway success when it was launched by Habitat. It re-creates the effect of a chandelier very simply using a delicate filigree of metal draped around a bulb. Manufacturer/outlet: *Habitat*

Taking the form of an open bell, this traditional-style wirework chandelier is illuminated by 18 candles. The graceful curves and the airiness of the design would make it a good focal point for an entrance hall or dining room. Manufacturer/outlet: *Marston and Langinger*

Donatello chandelier is inspired by eighteenth-century designs. The delicately entwined leaves are made out of ironwork with a rust finish. The handcrafted flowers are made of ivory-coloured porcelain. Manufacturer/outlet: *Louise Bradley*

A superb traditional crystal chandelier fitted with electrical candle bulbs. Such pieces are without question decorative showstoppers and a design as elaborate as this example would undoubtedly come in at the upper end of the price range. Manufacturer/outlet: *Wilkinson*

Colette chandelier features fuchsia-coloured glass drops. Colour adds an extra dimension to the branched, glittery form of the chandelier. Hanging a chandelier in a position where it will be reflected in a mirror multiplies the effect. Manufacturer/outlet: *Bombay Duck*

This delicate and pretty design featuring individually shaded bulbs would suit a variety of locations in the home. The armature is painted metal; the shades are either fabric- or raffia-covered and the drops are made of Murano glass. Manufacturer/outlet: *Baga*

85 Bulbs chandelier, designed by Rodi Graumans for Droog Design, is a contemporary classic in the making. The 'rose' where the individual cables meet is made out of plastic lighting connectors. This design is heavy and can be hung on a long drop. Manufacturer/outlet: *Dutchbydesign*

Decorative lights

This final category of light fitting runs the gamut from sculptural objects that are works of art in their own right to designs that stray into the realm of kitsch. Very few of these products produce enough light to carry out tasks effectively or even to boost the overall ambient levels appreciably. What they do deliver, however, is a great sense of vitality and playfulness that is always welcome. From lit objects, such as tables and stools, to the ever-popular fairy lights, decorative designs celebrate light in an evocative and joyful way.

Decorative or novelty lights are nothing new, but a greater range of designs is on the market now than in previous years, as technological developments permit ever more intriguing effects. While decorative lights are inherently attention-seeking, the low level of light they produce mean they rarely dominate. Many of these products are relatively inexpensive, so you can afford to succumb to impulse and rotate pieces in and out of view.

Firefly, by Emma Caselton, is a tubular standing light made of stainless steel and sandblasted glass and incorporating white LEDs. It comes in two heights. Manufacturer/outlet: *Innermost*

Still Life, designed by Carey + Chetiyawardana + Ossevoort, is a blank canvas that responds to stimuli. As you walk past, lights appear behind the canvas and follow your movement. If you use a mobile (cell) phone, the lights pulse. When multiple canvases are on display, the light jumps from canvas to canvas. Manufacturer/outlet: *Seen The Light*

Dunker light room dividers from IKEA consist of a canvas screen enclosing a metal framework inside which is concealed a number of light sources. Screens and dividers tend to block light as well as views; this design produces a soft ambient glow that dematerializes the form. Manufacturer/outlet: *IKEA*

Misspac, designed by Alvin Bagni, has a cheeky, animated form that was inspired by the computer game Pacman, popular in the 1980s. A lamp that is every bit as intriguing switched off as switched on, it is made of bright glazed ceramic. It can be used either as a table lamp or bedside lamp and emits a warm reddish glow. Manufacturer/outlet: *Habitat*

Pigeon light, designed by Ed Carpenter, is a cheerful light object, solid red when switched off, but with a glowing pink breast when lit. The bird can be stood on a table or perched on any suitable shelf or ledge using its clothes-peg feet. Manufacturer/outlet: *Thorsten van Elten*

Bubble, by Aaron Rincover, is a mobile light ball of soft silicone that you can take anywhere. It charges like a mobile (cell) phone, comes in a wide range of colours and lights up when you squeeze it. Manufacturer/outlet: *Mathmos*

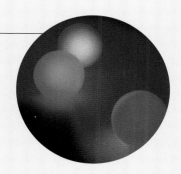

Light Reading, designed by Sam Johnston, is a particularly subtle and whimsical design. Made out of a special type of Perspex, the cover of the 'book' is matt black until the design is switched on, revealing the title on the spine. Manufacturer/outlet: *Thorsten van Elten*

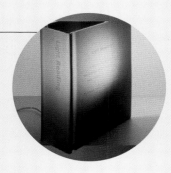

Glow Brick, designed by Alvaro Catalan de Ocon, is a light bulb filled with phosphor luminescent material and encased in acrylic. Once it is charged in natural daylight, it will glow for up to four hours in darkness. Manufacturer/outlet: *SUCK UK*

Dance is a light rope, a variant on the standard string of fairy lights. Here, the tiny individual bulbs are encased in a plastic sheath that can be safely strewn on any surface because very little heat is emitted. Manufacturer/outlet: *Habitat*

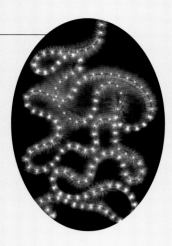

Spike wall light, designed by Tom Kirk, is a panel bristling with coloured plastic spikes, each lit by a tiny bulb that lasts up to 20,000 hours. Different single colours are available as well as a multicoloured version. Manufacturer/outlet: *Tom Kirk*

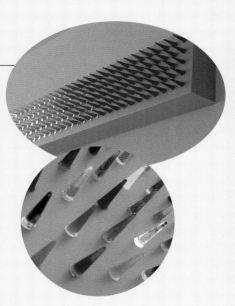

Boo!, designed by Christine Marchese and Ian Hume of Totem, is an interactive polyethylene stool with a suede top. If you sit on the stool, it lights up; when you stand up, the light goes out. The design is available in five colours. Manufacturer/outlet: *Aram*

Jack, designed by Tom Dixon in 1996, has been a great commercial success. The form is based on an overscaled jack. Made of polypropylene, the light is robust enough to sit on, and can also be stacked. It comes in a range of colours. Manufacturer/outlet: *Eurolounge*

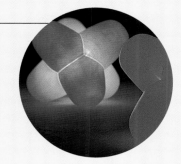

Light sources

A light fitting is a fixture or housing for a bulb or lamp. In technical terms, what makes the light itself is known as a 'light source'. Lighting designers and manufacturers often refer to the light fitting as the 'luminaire' and the bulb as the 'lamp'.

It is obviously important to make sure that you use the right bulb or lamp in a particular light fitting. While there may be a certain degree of interchangeability, the key factors to consider are the size and type of cap (bayonet, pin or screw) and the wattage. Never exceed the recommended wattage or there will be a risk of overheating the fitting or shade, causing scorching and possibly even a fire.

All domestic light sources are powered by electricity, but there are two principal ways in which light is produced: incandescence and fluorescence. In an incandescent lamp, the electricity passes through a filament to make it glow. In a fluorescent lamp, electricity passing through gas contained within the outer glass casing causes radiation that reacts with a phosphor coating to produce a glow.

In practice, the three principal types of light source most commonly used in the home today are tungsten, halogen and fluorescent, with tungsten still being far and away the most popular, although more modern developments such as fibre optics and LEDs are rapidly gaining ground for specific domestic applications. Each of these sources has its own advantages and disadvantages, in terms of energy efficiency, colour rendering and longevity.

Tungsten

The most familiar light source is the tungsten lamp, invented more than a century ago, and so-called because the filament inside the glass bulb or casing is made of tungsten. Electricity passed through the filament makes it glow. With repeated use, the filament gradually weakens, depositing evaporated metal on the inside of the bulb and blackening it. Eventually, when the filament can no longer carry the current, the bulb burns out.

PROS
• Tungsten lamps are cheap to replace and produce.
• The light bulbs are widely and easily available in many different outlets, from your local supermarkets to convenience stores.
• Tungsten lamps are easy to use and require no specialist gear. They run directly off mains electricity, respond instantly when switched on and are readily dimmable.
• No toxic chemicals are involved, so disposal is not problematic.
• Tungsten produces a warm, intimate light that is only slightly cooler than candlelight and renders colours well.
• Wattage ranges from 15 to 200 watts.
• There are a huge range of lamps available to suit a wide variety of light fittings, from the standard GLS (general lighting service) bulb to tubes, candle bulbs and PAR lamps (parabolic aluminized reflectors).
• Glass casing may be clear, pearl or tinted, which broadens the effects.

CONS

• Tungsten is the least energy-efficient of all light sources. More than 90 per cent of the energy these lamps consume is converted to heat, not light, which is why they are hot to touch. In turn, this makes them expensive to run.
• Lamps cannot be used close to flammable materials.
• With the exception of PAR lamps, lamps cannot be used outdoors, where sudden temperature variations might cause the thin glass casing to shatter.
• Tungsten lamps have the shortest life span of all light sources (1,000 hours if left on continuously; 2,000 hours in the case of PAR lamps). Switching them off and on frequently shortens the life span further.
• Tungsten is the least environmentally friendly light source.

Halogen

There are two main types of halogen lamp: mains-voltage and low-voltage. Like tungsten lamps, the filament within the lamp is made of tungsten; however, the introduction of halogen gas within the glass envelope results in a number of significant differences. The early uses of this type of light source were in shop displays, restaurants and theatres, but it is now increasingly common in the home, particularly in the low-voltage form, which requires a transformer to step the power down.

PROS OF MAINS-VOLTAGE HALOGEN

• Compared to ordinary tungsten lamps, the light that is emitted by a halogen lamp is much whiter and more sparkling, and is therefore closer to natural light. This makes it the ideal choice for use wherever fine colour judgements must be made, such as in kitchens or working areas.
• Halogen is instantly responsive, dimmable and needs no specialist gear. The bulb does not blacken over time.
• life span is about 3,000 hours, three times as long as ordinary tungsten.
• There is a range of lamp formats, from tubes to spots. Some of these incorporate dichroic reflectors.
• Wattages go up to 700 watts.

CONS OF MAINS-VOLTAGE HALOGEN

• Mains-voltage halogen is not energy-efficient and generates a considerable degree of heat.
• Lamps are not as widely available.
• Halogen lamps are more expensive to buy than tungsten lamps initially and they are just as expensive to run.
• Care must be taken to ensure the fitting is heatproof and that it is positioned where it will not pose a fire hazard (that is, away from flammable materials).

PROS OF LOW-VOLTAGE HALOGEN

• Low-voltage halogen provides the same crisp, white light as mains-voltage halogen.

• Lamps are very small, which means fittings are very discreet and light can be tightly focused to highlight displays.

• Wattages range from 15 to 50 watts.

• Because the lamps run on a much lower voltage, they are cheaper to run and will also generate less heat.

• The lamps have a life span of up to 3,500 hours.

CONS OF LOW-VOLTAGE HALOGEN

• A transformer is required to step the power down. While many of these are incorporated discreetly within the fitting, others are more overt and require concealment.

• Overuse of halogen spots can result in an ambience that is more retail than domestic.

• Care must be taken not to touch the lamps with bare hands, as grease from fingers can prevent the quartz envelope from functioning properly.

Fluorescent

Unlike incandescent light, fluorescent light is the product of the interaction between electrically charged gas and a phosphor coating lining the glass envelope or tube. In the past, fluorescent light was chiefly seen in commercial or industrial contexts; in the home, it was relegated to workshops, garages and other areas where aesthetic considerations were not relevant. Today, this light source has been much improved in terms of visual appearance, which has broadened its domestic application.

PROS

• Fluorescent lamps are relatively cheap to buy and have a long life span of up to 8,000 hours.

• They are very energy-efficient: for example, a 9-watt tube will generate as much light as a 40-watt tungsten bulb.

• These lamps generate very little heat, which means they can be safely used close to flammable materials or concealed behind baffles without a risk of fire. Fluorescents are ideal for architectural lighting.

• New compact and mini-fluorescent lamps are available with standard screw or bayonet caps and can be used in a wide range of fittings.

• Fluorescent tubes come in a number of colours. There are also 'warm' fluorescents that cast a less chilly light than the standard tube.

CONS

• Standard fluorescent tubes generate a cool light that has a greenish tinge. This makes them poor at rendering colours faithfully.

• The lamp does not burn out, but dims over time.

• The lamps contain toxic chemicals and must be disposed of carefully.

• Standard fluorescent lamps have a tendency to hum and flicker.

• New fluorescent lamps are dimmable, but expensive equipment is required. Compact fluorescents are not dimmable at all.

• There is generally a delay between switching on and the light coming on.

Fibre optics

While far from mainstream in its application, fibre optics is increasingly used for special effects in up-market lighting schemes. With this type of light, it is not the source itself that determines its characteristics, but the means by which the light is delivered. The source is a box situated remotely; the means of delivery is via thin strands of coated fibreglass or acrylic. Light is directed at one end of the bunched strands and emerges at the individual tips, which may be some distance away. The coating ensures that no light is emitted along the length of the strands; however, there are some types of fibre optics where the coating is omitted so that the overall effect is linear rather than starry.

PROS
• Fibre optics lighting creates dramatic decorative effects – starry ceilings or spangled floors; illuminated pools and running water.
• It is ideal for display lighting as it has a very low UV content. Delicate pictures or textiles will not be damaged.
• Because the light source is remote, fibre optics can be used to light water safely, both indoors and out.

CONS
• The chief disadvantage is expense.
• Fibre optics requires specialist installation.

LEDs

LEDs, or light-emitting diodes, have long been in use in display panels and electronic products such as computers and televisions. These tiny bulbs fit directly into an electrical circuit and are lit by the movement of electrons in semiconductor material. In recent years, they have increasingly been used in the home, both for practical and decorative lighting. Many designers believe that LEDs have the potential to replace low-voltage halogen in the not-too-distant future.

PROS
• LEDs give off hardly any heat because they have no filaments.
• They consume a mere 3 watts of energy but LEDs can produce as much light as an incandescent bulb.
• They last for incredibly long periods of time, between 50,000 and 100,000 hours.
• LEDs can be incorporated into wall or floor tiles.
• They can be used to illuminate water.

CONS
• The use of LEDs for general lighting is still in its infancy and light fittings are not, as yet,f widely available.
• Although LEDs are cheaper than they were previously, they are still expensive in comparison with other light sources.

Switches and controls

Lighting is controlled in many ways, from a basic on/off switch to sophisticated programmable systems. Choosing the method is a question of practicality, but stylistic issues come into play.

Wall switches

Fitted lights, such as pendants, wall lights, downlights and track lights, are generally controlled by wall switches. A wall switch may control only one light, for example, a central pendant, or it may control a lighting circuit, where individual table or floor lamps are plugged into a number of sockets around the room. This arrangement is common in the United States.

The common-or-garden wall switch is a white plastic plate inset with a rocker. Neat and unobtrusive, these are perfectly adequate, albeit a little uninspiring. Alternatives, which offer more in terms of style, include clear glass/plastic plates (ideal for mounting over decorative finishes you do not want to be interrupted); sleek brushed steel for a contemporary look; and brass or wooden switches for more traditional appeal. Instead of rockers, the controls may be toggles or knobs. Switches where the entire plate rocks and that can be operated by an elbow make practical sense in locations where your hands might be full or wet.

Pull-cords

In Britain wall switches are not permitted in bathrooms and lights are controlled either by a switch outside the door or by a pull-cord inside the bathroom. A number of decorative pulls are available, from turned wooden pulls to more whimsical designs.

Lamp switches

Light fittings designed to be plugged directly into a socket incorporate integral switches. These may be mounted on the lamp itself or fitted onto the flex, either a short distance from the lamp or (often in the case of standing lamps) in the form of a floor button designed to be controlled by the foot. In Britain the wall socket into which the fitting is plugged will have its own switch; elsewhere in the world, that is not the case. Many American floor and table lamps have integral switches that allow a dimmed option.

Dimmers

One of the simplest and most effective ways of improving existing lighting arrangements is to fit dimmer switches in place of standard controls. Most people tend to view dimmers as a means of changing the mood and ambience in living areas, but there are many other areas in the home that also benefit from this type of control. A dimmer switch enables you to

change the balance between background lighting, local light and natural light according to the time of day and the activities that are taking place within a given area. In multipurpose spaces, such as open-plan kitchen and eating areas, dimmers enable you to raise the light level when you are preparing food and lower it again when you are eating.

Dimmers are widely available and easy to fit. They work by reducing the power to the light source and in the process they extend the life of filament bulbs or lamps by a considerable degree. All tungsten and halogen lamps can be dimmed. Some low-voltage lamps are not dimmable, however, and neither are compact fluorescents. Standard fluorescent tubes can only be dimmed with expensive gear. Dimmers generally can only be used to control a couple of lights and most incorporate an on-off switch.

Open-door switches

These switches, the most basic of the automatic variety, are mounted inside the doors of fitted wardrobes, closets or fridges to activate an internal light when the door is opened.

Timers

Putting lights on timers is a proven way of deterring intruders when you are away from home. The simplest timing device plugs straight into a wall socket and controls the light that is powered by that outlet. A number of timers can be set to trigger lights at set intervals in different parts of the home. More sophisticated timers function in a similar way to heating thermostats, while computer-controlled panels also allow you to preset lighting times.

Approach lighting

External lights can be controlled by heat or motion sensors that trigger the light when someone approaches. Like timers, approach lighting is chiefly a security measure, but it also provides an economic way of delivering light for a short period outside entrances so that you can find your way safely indoors. Some approach lighting systems are triggered when an infrared beam is interrupted; these work in a similar way to burglar alarms.

Computer controls

'Intelligent' lighting systems provide you with a centrally positioned panel that programmes and controls lighting throughout the home. Colourwashing lighting systems are often operated in such a fashion, using a hand-held controller. Lights can be preset to come on or go off at certain times or to dim or brighten according to ambient light levels.

Practicalities

Safety is of paramount consideration when planning any alteration to existing lighting arrangements. Installing fixed lights, such as downlights or track lighting, putting in new sockets or circuits, or routing cabling to external lighting are jobs for a qualified professional who is a member of an accredited national organization. If you decide to put up some shelves and bodge the job, the worst thing that can happen is that they will fall down. If you tinker with electricity without knowing what you're doing, your life and your home are at serious risk. A badly wired plug is enough to start a fire.

Indoor installations

Depending on where you live, electricity is supplied to your home in a number of different ways. In Britain the standard arrangement consists of a number of fused ring circuits that take power from the distribution box to wall sockets and then back again. Individual spurs may also extend from the ring circuits. Elsewhere in the world, radial circuits are more common. These fan out from the distribution box and terminate at the last socket.

Power circuits take power to individual wall sockets for plug-in appliances and light fittings such as table lamps, standing lamps and desk lamps. As well as power sockets, many homes also have separate lighting circuits, which take a smaller load. These are typically radial and take power to ceiling-mounted fittings and fixtures that are controlled by a wall switch.

If you want to increase the number of lights in a given area, you may need to install either more wall sockets or an extra circuit. Additional circuits will allow for greater flexibility and provide the opportunity to group lighting controls so that a number of lights can be switched on and off at one time at a convenient location.

Outdoor installations

External lighting varies in complexity and scale but all installations, however small and simple, should be carried out by a professional. There are three main types of installation: mains voltage, low voltage and a combination of the two.

Mains-voltage installations take power from the distribution box sited indoors to external waterproof fittings. Special heavy-duty cabling is used, buried in plastic conduits or in channels at least 45cm (18in) below the ground. Routing of cabling is critical and conduits must not be sited in areas that are likely to be disturbed by digging (whether by human or animal). If there is a risk that such a disturbance is likely, the cabling should be buried at a much greater depth. If you will also be using the system to take power to an external building, such as a shed or greenhouse, you may need a separate distribution box to cope with the additional load of running appliances such as lawnmowers and power tools.

Low-voltage installations require transformers to step the power down to 12 volts. A single transformer may be used to serve a number of fittings (the maximum safe number will be specified in terms of rating); alternatively, individual fittings may have their own

integral transformers. Because the cabling takes only a low voltage, it does not need to be buried, although it must be heatproof, and it must still be sited where it will not present a trip hazard, and where it is not likely to come in contact with the blades of a lawnmower or of other cutting tools, such as secateurs or shears.

There is a wide range of fittings suitable for external use, all of which are designed to be waterproof. The IP or Ingress Protection code specifies the degree to which a fitting is resistant to water and dust. Outdoor sockets should also be waterproof and covered.

Energy-saving strategies

Lighting accounts for between 10 and 15 per cent of the electricity consumed in every home. By making a few simple substitutions and changing your day-to-day habits, you can reduce that amount by up to 80 per cent, saving money on your power bills and helping to ease the pressures on the environment caused by carbon dioxide emissions.

• Don't leave lights burning in unoccupied rooms. Switch them off.
• Keep bulbs and shades clean. Wipe reflectors from time to time so that dust does not build up and reduce the amount of reflected light.
• Make the most of natural light to reduce reliance on artificial sources. Keep window treatments simple; opt for blinds or curtains that pull well clear of the glass to allow maximum daylight through. Using light-toned surfaces and finishes in rooms helps to spread any available natural light around.
• Focus artificial light right where you need it and keep background light at a lower level.
• Opt for a low wattage.
• Put tungsten and halogen lamps on dimmer controls to reduce the power input.
• Use timers and sensors for external lighting.
• In the areas where you spend most time, substitute CFLs (compact fluorescent lamps) for standard tungsten or halogen bulbs. CFLs last ten times longer and consume 75 per cent less electricity than filament bulbs, which convert most of the energy they consume to heat. CFLs now come in a wide range of shapes and sizes and with bayonet or screw caps so they can be used in many different types of light fitting. The only disadvantage is that they cannot be used in conjunction with dimmers, sensors or timers.

Safety

Both domestic electrical supply and the design and manufacture of light fittings and lamps are subject to strict controls and regulations, stricter in some parts of the world than in others. You should always err on the side of safety when it comes to electrical work and lighting installation. All work must be carried out by a reputable electrician who is a member of an officially recognized organization to ensure a safe set-up.

GENERAL

• Make sure your lighting infrastructure is safe and up to date. Signs of trouble include fuses that blow frequently and for no good reason. Wiring that is more than 20 years old will probably require replacement. If you suspect your wiring is out of date, ask an electrician to test the system for you.

• Fraying flexes can cause electric shocks or fire. Replace any flexes where the sheathing is worn through.

• With time, plastic bulb-holders can become brittle and break, and metal bulb-holders can become bent and twisted, which means there is not a proper contact between the bulb and the power source. Replace any broken bulb-holders to avoid shock or fire.

• Overloaded sockets are a hazard. Ask an electrician to install more sockets for you rather than increase the load on a single socket with extension cables. Alternatively, you may need another power circuit to serve your needs.

• New light fittings must pass stringent safety standards. The same is not the case when it comes to period or retro lights that you might buy at a junk shop or secondhand outlet. If you buy an old fitting, have it checked over by an electrician to make sure it is safe to operate.

• All new light fittings are labelled to show the recommended wattage of bulb that should be used in conjunction with them. Never exceed that wattage or you may run the risk of causing a fire by overheating.

• When changing bulbs, make sure the light is switched off. Never change bulbs with wet hands. Allow the bulb to cool down first so that you don't burn your fingers. Halogen lamps should never be touched with bare hands, as the grease from your fingers can interfere with the way the quartz envelope functions.

• Make sure plugs are correctly wired and fitted with the appropriate fuse. If you don't know how to change a plug, get someone to do it for you. Loose wires can cause fires.

• Transformers are individually rated according to how many lights they can support. A 100-watt transformer, for example, will be able to support four 25-watt lamps. Never exceed the rating. Transformers should be placed in dry, well-ventilated areas.

• Keep lights well away from flammable materials, such as paper, card, fabric or wood. Filament lamps, such as tungsten and halogen, give off a great deal of heat. Fairy lights and fluorescents can be used in closer proximity to flammable materials with no risk.

• Do not allow flexes to trail across the floor where they might trip someone up.

• Recessed fittings, such as downlights, need an adequate ceiling void to allow for ventilation and prevent overheating. In old houses, there may be a build-up of dust and dirt in the ceiling space that could pose a fire hazard. Always have recessed or fixed lights installed by a professional, who will ensure the space is clear.

• Keep bulbs and fittings clean, free of dust, dirt and grease. When replacing or maintaining bulbs and fittings in awkward or high locations, always use a stable ladder and get someone to steady it for you.

CIRCULATION AREAS

• Light staircases so that it is clear where the treads and risers are to prevent accidental tumbles. Avoid lights that throw confusing shadows.

• Switches should be positioned by the entrance door and at the top and bottom of the stairs.

• Avoid freestanding lights or lights with flexes in cramped halls, and on stairs and landings.

• Position lights carefully to avoid glare.

KITCHENS

• Positioning of lights is critical in working areas of the kitchen, where you will be coming into contact with sharp knives, heat sources and pans of boiling water. Light the counter, worktop and hob so that you are not standing in your own shadow. Make sure there is no glare reflecting off shiny surfaces that might momentarily dazzle you.

• Avoid trailing flexes and freestanding lights.

• Don't overload sockets.

• Keep lamps and fittings clear of grease and dust.

• In wet areas, near the sink, make sure lights are fully enclosed so there is no risk of the bulb shattering if it is splashed by water.

BATHROOMS

• Regulations vary from country to country with respect to bathroom light fittings and controls. In Britain, for example, all bathroom lights must be controlled either by a switch located outside the room or by a pull-cord within the room. Unless fittings are completely enclosed, with no exposed metal parts or bulbs, they must not be positioned any nearer than 2.5m (8ft) to any sinks, showers or tubs.

• Special lights are produced for use in showers and wet rooms. Check that such fittings conform to safety regulations and housings are fully waterproof.

• Avoid low pendant fixtures that leave the bulb exposed where it might be splashed or knocked into and shatter.

• Never readjust the position of light fittings with wet hands.

WORKROOMS

• Provide focused, bright light targeted at the work surface to avoid eyestrain. For computer work, combine uplighting with adjustable task light directed at the keyboard.

• Task light is also required for workshops or any areas where you will be using sharp tools and machinery. Avoid obscuring shadows and provide a good level of general background light as well as directional light.

CHILDREN'S ROOMS AND PLAYROOMS

• Freestanding floor lamps should be avoided in these areas, since flexes may be tripped over or tugged.

• Make sure table lamps are securely anchored, with flexes tucked well out of the way.

• Fit socket covers to power points. Many children are tempted to poke sharp objects, such as keys, into sockets.

• Decorative lights and carousels are objects of considerable fascination. Either position them where they cannot be interfered with or supervise their use.

EXTERNAL LIGHTING

• All external installations should be carried out by a professional.

• Choose waterproof fittings specifically designed for outdoor use.

• Do not overload the transformers if you are installing low-voltage lighting. Position transformers carefully, according to the manufacturer's recommendations.

• Keep fittings clear of leaves and other debris.

• Make sure cabling is robust and buried if necessary.

Stockists and suppliers

LIGHTING SHOWROOMS & SPECIALIST RETAILERS

For a comprehensive view on what's available, visit one of the outlets dedicated solely to lighting. Many of these stock a range of designs, both traditional and contemporary, and many offer design services as well as a supply of individual fittings.

Cameron Peters
The Old Dairy, Home Farm,
Ardington, Wantage OX12 8PD, UK
+44 (0)1235 835 000
www.cameronpeters.co.uk
The widest selection of fine lighting in the UK, traditional and contemporary. More than 60 suppliers (including Cini & Nils, Fontana Arte, Flos, Diffuse). Consultation and design service available, as well as bespoke.

Christopher Wray
591–3 King's Road, London
SW6 2YW, UK
+44 (0)20 7751 8701
www.christopher-wray.com
Large selection of traditional lighting, with a separate showroom specializing in contemporary designs.

Crystal Lighting Centre
+44 (0)1280 860 154
www.crystal-lighting-centre.com
Crystal downlights, spots, fibre optics and panels, designed and manufactured in Austria by Swarovski.

Electrics Lighting and Design
530 West Francisco Blvd,
San Rafael, CA 94901, USA
+1 415 258 9996
www.electrics.com
Wide range of modern Italian lighting.

Hector Finch Lighting
90 Wandsworth Bridge Road,
London SW6 2TF, UK
+44 (0)20 7731 8886
www.hectorfinch.com
Antique lighting fixtures.

John Cullen Lighting
585 King's Road, London
SW6 2EH, UK
+44 (0)20 7371 5400
www.johncullenlighting.co.uk
Modern light fittings and individual design service.

Kichler Lighting Group
7711 East Pleasant Valley Road,
PO Box 318010, Cleveland,
OH 44131-8010, UK
www.kichler.com
Comprehensive range of lighting.

Lightbox Limited
Beaumont Building, Great Ducie Street, Manchester M3 1PQ, UK
+44 (0)161 832 9334
www.lightboxstores.com

Lightforms
168 Eighth Avenue, New York,
NY 10011, UK
+1 212 255 4664
www.lightformsinc.com
Contemporary lamps and lampshades.

The Lighting Center Ltd
240 East 59th Street, New York,
NY 10022, USA
+1 212 888 8380
www.lightingcenter-ny.com
Lamps, recessed and track fittings.

Lightolier
631 Airport Road, Fall River,
MA 02720, USA
+1 508 679 8131
www.lightolier.com
Contemporary lighting range.

London Lighting Company
135 Fulham Road, London
SW3 6RT, UK
+44 (0)20 7589 3612
www.londonlighting.co.uk
Modern light fittings.

M S K Illumination, Inc
235 East 57th Street, New York,
NY 10022, USA
+1 212 888 6474
www.mskillumination.com
Comprehensive range of fittings.

Original BTC Ltd
Old Rectory, Church Hanborough,
Oxfordshire, OX8 8AB, UK
+44 (0)1993 882 251
Good range of light fittings.

SKK
34 Lexington Street, London
W1F 0LH, UK
+44 (0)20 7434 4095
www.skk.net
Innovative designs and lighting consultancy.

SHOPS & DEPARTMENT STORES

Many department stores and retail chains feature lighting departments that offer a range of different types of fitting. Individual stores also stock lighting alongside furniture ranges.

ABC Carpet & Home
888 Broadway, New York,
NY 10003, USA
+1 212 473 3000
www.abchome.com
Home emporium stocking hundreds of fittings; stores throughout the USA.

Aram
110 Drury Lane, London
WC2B 5SG, UK
+44 (0)20 7557 7557
www.aram.co.uk
Designs from contemporary manufacturers such as Flos and Luceplan.

Aspects
+44 (0)113 201 8888
www.aspectsinternational.com
Contemporary Danish designs.

Bed, Bath & Beyond
+1 800 462 3966
www.bedbathandbeyond.com
Branches throughout the USA offering a wide range of lighting.

Bombay Duck
+44 (0)20 8749 3000
www.bombayduck.co.uk
Asian-inspired designs.

The Conran Shop
Michelin House, 81 Fulham Road,
London SW3 6RD, UK
+44 (0)20 7589 7401

Bridgemarket, 407 East 59th Street,
New York, NY 10022, USA
+1 212 755 9079
www.conran.com
Contemporary lighting and furniture; see website for details of other Conran Shops.

Crate & Barrel
+1 800 967 6696
www.crateandbarrel.com
Branches throughout the USA.

Debenhams
334–8 Oxford Street, London
W1C 1JG, UK
+44 (0)20 7580 3000
www.debenhams.com
Stores throughout the UK. Good selection of mass-market light fittings.

Habitat
196 Tottenham Court Road,
London W1P 7LG, UK
+44 (0)20 7631 3880
www.habitat.net
Exciting lighting department, including many decorative designs.

Heal's
The Heal's Building, 196 Tottenham Court Road, London W1T 7LQ, UK
+44 (0)20 7636 1666
www.heals.co.uk
Contemporary lighting.

IKEA
www.ikea.com
www.ikea.co.uk
Swedish superstores with extensive lighting range.

Jim Lawrence
+44 (0)1206 263 459
www.jim-lawrence.co.uk
Traditional ironwork.

John Lewis
Oxford Street, London
W1A 1EX, UK
+44 (0)20 7629 7711
www.johnlewis.com
Branches throughout the UK. Selection of traditional and contemporary fittings.

Knoll
1235 Water Street, East Greenville,
PA 18041, USA
+1 800 343 5665
www.knoll.com
Contemporary fittings from leading modern designers.

Louise Bradley
15 Walton Street, London
SW3 2HX, UK
+44 (0)20 7589 1442
Contemporary lighting and furniture.

Marston and Langinger
192 Ebury Street, London
SW1W 8UP, UK
+44 (0)20 7881 5717

117 Mercer Street, New York,
NY 10012, USA
+1 212 965 0434
www.marston-and-langinger.com
Chandeliers, lanterns and sconces.

Niedermaier
400 North Oakley Blvd, Chicago,
IL 60612, USA
+ 1 312 492 9400
www.niedermaier.com
Table and floor lamps.

Pottery Barn
+1 888 779 5176
www.potterybarn.com
Branches throughout the USA.

Purves & Purves
222 Tottenham Court Road,
London W1T 7PZ, UK
+44 (0)20 7580 8223
www.purves.co.uk
Contemporary designs.

Restoration Hardware
+1 800 762 1005
www.restorationhardware.com
Branches throughout the USA.

SCP
135–9 Curtain Road, London
EC2A 3BX, UK
+44 (0)20 7739 1869
www.scp.co.uk
Fittings by leading modern designers.

Skandium
86 Marylebone High Street,
London W1U 4QT, UK
+44 (0)20 7935 2077
www.skandium.com
Specialists in Scandinavian design.

Thorsten van Elten
22 Warren Street, London
W1T 5LU, UK
+44 (0)20 7388 8008
www.thorstenvanelten.com
*Contemporary decorative lights including
'Pigeon' light and 'Light Reading'.*

Vaughan
G1 Chelsea Harbour Design
Centre, London SW10 0XE, UK
+44 (0)20 7349 4600

D & D Building – Suite 1511,
979 Third Avenue, New York,
NY 10022, USA
+1 212 319 7070
www.vaughandesigns.com
Wide range of reproduction fittings.

Viaduct
1–10 Summers Street, London
EC1R 5BD, UK
+44 (0)20 7278 8456
www.viaduct.co.uk
Fittings by leading modern designers.

Wilkinson
1 Grafton Street, London
W1S 4EA, UK
+44 (0)20 7495 2477
www.wilkinson-plc.com
*Reproduction chandeliers;
chandelier restorer.*

MANUFACTURERS, DESIGNERS & OUTLETS
Contact individual manufacturers
or designers for details of stockists
and suppliers in your area.

2pm
+44 (0)20 8965 9510
www.2pm.co.uk
*Innovative lighting designs, including
'Wineglass' chandelier.*

Anglepoise
+44 (0)2392 250 934
www.anglepoise.com
The classic task light.

Arc Lighting
+44 (0)1983 523 399
www.arclighting.com
Illuminated wall tiles.

Artemide
www.artemide.com
*One of the leading Italian
manufacturers of contemporary lighting.*

Baga
www.baga.it
Italian lighting designs.

Best & Lloyd
+44 (0)121 455 6400
www.bestlite.com
Classic Bestlite and others made to order.

Castlight
www.castlight.co.uk
Porcelain fittings by Margaret O'Rorke.

Cini & Nils
+39 02 334 3071
www.cinienils.com
Modern lighting systems and track.

Dernier & Hamlyn
+44 (0)20 8760 0900
www.dernier-hamlyn.com
Historic and contemporary lighting.

Diffuse
+44 (0)1462 638 331
www.diffuse.co.uk
Porcelian light fittings.

Dutchbydesign
+44 (0)8707 446 478
www.dutchbydesign.co.uk
Designs by Mooi and Materialise.

Flos
www.flos.net
*Contemporary lighting designs by
Castiglioni, Starck, Citterio, Morrison.*

Fontana Arte
www.fontanaarte.it
Leading Italian lighting manufacturer.

Foscarini
+39 041 595 3811
www.foscarini.com
Contemporary lighting.

Ingo Maurer
www.ingo-maurer.com
Renowed German lighting designer.

Innermost
+44 (0)20 8451 3320
www.innermost.co.uk
Designs such as 'Hugging' and 'Mr Bigoli'.

Kartell
www.kartell.it
Contemporary plastic light fittings.

Le Klint
www.leklint.com
Danish hand-folded pendants and shades.

LIGHT
www.light.be
Contemporary designs.

Loop
+44 (0)7792 474 091
www.loop.ph
'Digital Dawn Blind'.

Louis Poulsen
www.louis-poulsen.com
*Danish lighting manufacturers
and producers of PH luminaires
by Poul Henningsen.*

Luceplan
www.luceplan.com
Contemporary home and office lighting.

Mathmos
+44 (0)20 7549 2700
www.mathmos.com
Lava lamps and other decorative fittings.

McCloud & Co
+44 (0)1373 813 600
www.mccloud.co.uk
*Table lamps and chandeliers designed
by Kevin McCloud.*

Mediterraneo
+44 (0)20 7720 6556
www.mediterraneodesign.com
Bespoke Venetian chandeliers.

Metalarte
+34 93 477 0069
www.metalarte.com
Serrano waterproof lights.

Noguchi Museum
+1 718 721 2308
www.noguchi.org
'Akari' lanterns by Noguchi.

Oluce
+39 29 849 1435
www.oluce.com
Track, recessed and pendant fittings.

Pallucco
+39 0422 438 800
www.pallucco.com
Lamps and contemporary light fittings.

Paul Cocksedge
+44 (0)7966 790 998
www.paulcocksedge.co.uk
Innovative British lighting designer.

Secto
+35 89 505 0598
www.sectodesign.fi
Finnish designers various fittings.

Seen the Light
www.seenthelight.org
Contemporary designs.

Studio Tord Boontje
www.tordboontje.com
'Wednesday' light, among other designs.

Swarovski
www.swarovski.com
Austrian crystal chandeliers.

Suck UK
+44 (0)20 7923 0011
www.suck.uk.com
Designs include 'Glow Brick'.

Tecnolumen
www.tecnolumen.de
Re-editions of Bauhaus designs.

Tom Dixon
+44 (0)20 7400 0500
www.tomdixon.net
Designer of 'Jack' light.

Tom Kirk
+44 (0)20 8766 6715
www.tomkirk.com
'Spike' lamp.

Totem
+44 (0)20 7243 0692
www.totem-uk.com
Designers of 'Boo!' light-up stool.

Venini
+39 041 273 7204
www.venini.com
Leading makers of Murano blown glass.

Index

Photographic acknowledgments

The publisher would like to thank the following photographers, agencies and companies for their kind permission to reproduce the following photographs in this book:

2–4 James Morris/The Interior Archive (Architect: Claudio Silvestrin); 6–7 Lewis Whyld/ SWNS (Art installation by Richard Box); 9 Solo Syndication courtesy neugerriemschneider, Berlin and Tanya Bonakdar gallery, New York; 10 Geoffrey Clements/Corbis (© Estate of Dan Flavin/ARS, NY and DACS, London 2005); 11 Jerome Galland/Aleph/Marie Claire Maison; 12 Simon Kwong/Reuters; 13 Damian Russell/Elle Decoration (Stylist: Amanda Koster); 17 Ray Main/Mainstream (Bailey Home & Garden); 18 Ray Main/Mainstream; 19 Luke White/The Interior Archive (Designer: Caroline Gardner); 20 Ray Main/Mainstream; 21 Andreas von Einsiedel (Interior designer: Alex Michaelis); 23 Ray Main/Mainstream; 24 Ake E:son Lindman (Architect: Shideh Shaygan); 25 Paul Massey/ Mainstream (Architect: John Pawson); 26 Ray Main/Mainstream; 27 Ray Main/Mainstream (Designer: Claire Nash); 28 Vercruysse and Dujardin (Architects: bob361); 29 Ray Main/Mainstream (Chateau De Massillan); 30 Warren Smith/Red Cover (Architect: Gavin Jackson); 31 Ray Main/Mainstream; 32 above Ray Main/Mainstream (Architect: Littman Goddard Hogarth); 32 centre Tim Beddow/The Interior Archive (Architect: McCullough Malvin); 32 below Ray Main/ Mainstream; 33 Ake E:son Lindman (Architect: Nosuch Architects); 34 Courtesy of Margaret O'Rorke; 35 above Morley von Sternberg (Architect: MAE Architects); 35 below Stellan Herner; 36 Richard Powers (Architects: Carnachan Architects); 37 Giorgio Possenti/ Vega MG; 38 above Andreas von Einsiedel (Architects: 3s Architects); 38 below Ray Main/Mainstream (Designer: Jo Warman); 39 left Nicholas Kane/Arcaid (Architect: Buschow Henley); 39 right Simon Upton/ The Interior Archive (Architect: Julian Powell-Tuck); 40 Winfried

Heinze/Red Cover; 40–1 James Morris/The Interior Archive (Designer: Sarah Pavey); 41 Luke White/The Interior Archive (Designer: John Ashwell); 42 Alexander van Berge/Taverne Agency/Elle Wonen; 42–3 Paul Tyagi/View (Architect: Enclosure); 44 Guy Obijn; 45 Jan Baldwin/Narratives; 46–53 Chris Tubbs/Conran Octopus (Architect: Richard Neal); 57 Richard Powers (Architect: Andrew Lister); 58–9 Guglielmo Galvin/Red Cover; 60–1 John Hall/Photozest/Inside (Architect: Page Goolrick); 62 Richard Powers (Architect: Carnachan Architects); 65 David Brittain/Homes & Gardens/IPC Syndication; 66 Caroline Arber/Homes & Gardens/IPC Syndication; 67 Bruno Helbling (Architect: Gus Wustemann); 68 Luke White/The Interior Archive (Architect: David Kelman); 69 Chris Tubbs/Red Cover (Architect: Ian Hogarth); 71 James Mitchell/Red Cover; 73 Paul Tyagi/View (Architect: Enclosure); 74 Ray Main/Mainstream; 75 Dook/Photozest/Inside/H&L; 77 Marie-Jose Jarry/Marie Claire Maison; 78 Edina van der Wyck/The Interior Archive (Designer: Marion Cotterill); 78–9 Allan Crow/View (Architect: 51% Studios); 79 Richard Powers (Architect: Alex Smith); 80–1 Grey Crawford/Red Cover (Architect: Steven Ehrlich); 82 James Silverman/Red Cover (Architect: Jonas Lindvall); 83 left Hans Zeeger/Taverne Agency (Stylist: Marianne Wermenbol); 83 right Grazia Ike Branco; 85 Richard Powers (Architect: Abigail Turin); 86–7 Helen Fickling; 87 Guy Obijn; 88–9 Ray Main/Mainstream (Andrew Weaving/20th Century Design); 90 left Courtesy of Ron Arad & Associates Ltd., Designed by Ron Arad, 2001 (In June 2004 Ron Arad was made aware of Bill Culbert's 'Cubic Projection' dated 1968, an undisputed precedent to his I.P.C.O from 2001); 90–1 Earl Carter/Taverne Agency (Stylist: Annemarie Kiely); 91 right Vercruysse and Dujardin; 92–3 David Ross/Visi/Camera Press; 94 Richard Powers (Architect: Marmol Radziner; Interior Design: Carole Katleman); 96 left David George/Beth Coyne Agency; 96 right Jan Baldwin/Narratives; 97

M. Hoyle/Photozest/Inside/H&L; 98 above Ake E:son Lindman (Architect: Claesson Koivisto Rune); 98 below Ray Main/Mainstream (Designer: Jo Warman); 99 Richard Davies (Architect: John Pawson); 100 Richard Glover/View (Architect: Reading & West Architects); 100–1 Ake E:son Lindman (Architect: Shideh Shaygan); 102 above Richard Powers (Architect: Carnachan Architects); 102 below Andreas von Einsiedel (Architect: David Miller, Interior Designer: Simon Dobson Space); 103 Serge Brison (Architect: Bureau Claisse & Associates); 106 Alexander van Berge/Taverne Agency (Stylist: Ulrika Lundgren; Chandelier: Brand en van Egmond); 107 Ray Main/Mainstream (Designer: Teijo Remy); 108 John Dummer/Taverne Agency (Stylist: Yvonne Bakker); 109 Fritz von der Schulenburg/The Interior Archive (Designers: Jasper Conran and Ann Boyd Associates); 111 Sveinung Brathen; 112 above Adrian Briscoe/Elle Decoration; 112 below Anders Bergh/House of Pictures; 113 Maarten Schets © Sanoma Uitgevers; 114 Eric Flogny/Aleph/Marie Claire Maison; 115 Adrian Briscoe/Elle Decoration (Stylist: Amanda Smith); 116 Ray Main/Mainstream; 117 Tim Evan-Cook/Red Cover (Designer: Matthew Williamson); 118 Cedric Martigny/Marie Claire Maison; 119 above Iben Ahlberg/Home Sweet Home Co.; 119 below Earl Carter/Living Etc/IPC Syndication; 120–1 Matt Chisnall/Courtesy of Allford Hall Monaghan Morris Architects (Lighting designer: Martin Richman); 122 above Mary Wadsworth/Living Etc/IPC Syndication; 122 below left Fritz von der Schulenburg/The Interior Archive; 122 below right Adrian Briscoe/Essentials/IPC Syndication; 123 Tom Vack/Ingo Maurer GmbH (Design by Ingo Maurer, 2003); 124 Richard Brine/Courtesy of Paul Cocksedge; 125 left Ray Main/Mainstream; 125 right Maarten Schets © Sanoma Uitgevers; 126 Winfried Heinze/Elle Decoration (Stylist: Alex Teal); 127–8 Ray Main/Mainstream; 128 below Bruno Helbling/Zapaimages; 129 above left and above right Tecnolumen (Design: Nico Heilmann, 2003); 129 below left Innermost; 129 below right

Courtesy of Margaret O'Rorke; 130 Dook/Photozest/Inside/H&L; 131 Ake E:son Lindman (Architect: John Robert Nilsson); 132 Vercruysse and Dujardin (Modular lighting instruments tks); 133 above Nick Hufton/View (Architect: Jonathan Clark); 133 below Richard Powers; 134 left Guy Obijn; 134 right and 135 Courtesy of Rachel Wingfield/loop.pH Ltd; 136 Artecnica; 137 Chris Tubbs/Conran Octopus; 138–9 Vincent Knapp (Interior Designer: Gerald Schmorl); 140 left S. Anton/Photozest/Inside (Stylist: C. Exelmans); 140 right P. Baasch/Photozest/Inside/H&L; 141 Fritz von der Schulenburg/The Interior Archive (Architect: Paula Navone); 142 Birgitta Wolfgang Drejer/House of Pictures; 143 Dana Gallagher/Philippe Achard; 144 Cristobal Palma (Architect: Julie Richards Architectural Design Ltd.); 145 courtesy of Kai Piippo; 146 left Philip Sowells/Digital Home Magazine; 146 right and 147 Christian Banfield/Courtesy of Andy Martin Associates (Lighting Designer: Kate Wilkins); 148 Metalarte (Designed by Hector Serrano); 149 S. Clement/Photozest/Inside (Stylist: M. Radot); 150 Ray Main/Mainstream; 151 Mel Yates/Elle Decoration; 152–3 Courtesy of Isometrix Lighting & Design; 154 above and centre Ray Main/Mainstream (Artwork: 'Microchrome' by Jeremy Lord); 154 below Bruno Helbling/Zapaimages; 155 Minh + Wass (Interior Designer: David Khouri); 156–7 Anson Smart; 157 Deidi von Schaewen (Owner: Ralph Weiden); 184 Dennis Gilbert/View (Architect: Brady Mallalieu); 192 Max Zambelli/Elle Decoration

Every effort has been made to trace the copyright holders. We apologize in advance for any unintentional omissions and would be pleased to insert the appropriate acknowledgement in any subsequent publication.

With thanks to the following shops and manufacturers for kindly supplying the pictures for 'The Compendium'. Pictures on each page are numbered from left to right, top to bottom.

Alberto Meda 162, no.1; Matilde Alessandro 163, no.8; Anglepoise 162, no.2; Aram 169, no.8, 173, no.7; Artecnica 169, no.4; Aspects International 170, no.4; Bombay Duck 171, no.6; Cameron Peters (Baga 165, no.5, 171, no.7; Cini & Nils 161, nos.1, 3 & 5; Diffuse 160, no.2; Flos 160, no.4, 162, nos.3 & 4, 163, no.4, 165, no.6, 166, nos.2 & 4, 167, nos.1, 2, 4 & 6, 168, no.4, 169, no.1, 170, no.2; Fontana Arte 160, no.1, 163, nos.2, 3 & 6, 164, no.2, 165, nos.3, 7 & 8, 166, no.1, 168, nos.2 & 3; Louis Poulsen 165, nos.2 & 4, 167, no.8, 169, no.6; Materialise 166, no.3; O Luce 167, no.5; Pallucco 161, no.8, 167, no.3; Secto 163, no.5 and Wilkinson 171, no.5); Paul Cocksedge/photo: © Richard Brine 2005 169, no.3; Conran Octopus/Thomas Stewart 173, no.8; The Crystal Lighting Centre 161, no.7; Debenhams 164, no.1; Dutchbydesign 168, no.1; Foscarini 165, no.1; Habitat 160, no.3, 161, nos.2 & 4, 167, no.7, 169, no.5, 171, nos.1 & 2, 172, no.3, 173, no.5; Ikea 161, no.6, 172, no.4; Innermost Limited 169, no.2, 172, no.1; Jim Lawrence 170, no.3; Kartell 164, no.4; Louise Bradley 171, no.4; Marston & Langinger 171, no.3; Mathmos 173, no.2; Original BTC 163, no.7; SCP Limited 171, no.8; Seen the light 172, no.2; Skandium 169, no.7; Suck UK 173, no.4; Tecnolumen 164, no.3; Thorsten van Elten/photo: © Lara Gosling & Louise Melchoir 173, no.1; Thorsten van Elten 173, no.3; Totem Design Ltd 173, no.7; 2pm 170, no.1; Vaughan Limited 163, no.1

Author's acknowlegments

I would like to thank Zia Mattocks, Liz Boyd, Lucy Gowans, and all the team at Conran Octopus for their brilliant support and grace under pressure. A very special thank you to Jenny Hall of Jenny Hall Communications and to Peter and Cheryl Younie of Cameron Peters for taking the time to give us an illuminating and inspirational day at their showroom.